the SKATE BOARDING field manual

Ryan Stutt

FIREFLY BOOKS

A FIREFLY BOOK

Published by Firefly Books Ltd. 2009

First printing

Publisher Cataloging-in-Publication Data (U.S.)
Stutt, Ryan.
   The skateboard field manual / Ryan Stutt.
[ ] p. : ill., col. photos. ; cm.
Includes index.
Summary: An illustrated guide to learning and improving skateboarding skill
and technique, plus a brief overview of skateboarding culture and history.
ISBN-13: 978-1-55407-362-7 (pbk.) ISBN-10: 1-55407-362-6 (pbk.)
ISBN-13: 978-1-55407-467-9 (bound) ISBN-10: 1-55407-467-3 (bound)
1. Skateboarding. I. Title.
796.22 dc22   GV859.8.S788 2009

Library and Archives Canada Cataloguing in Publication
Stutt, Ryan
   The skateboard field manual / Ryan Stutt.
Includes index.
ISBN-13: 978-1-55407-362-7 (pbk.) ISBN-10: 1-55407-362-6 (pbk.)
ISBN-13: 978-1-55407-467-9 (bound) ISBN-10: 1-55407-467-3 (bound)
1. Skateboarding--Juvenile literature. I. Title.
GV859.8.S88 2009   j796.22   C2008-904863-6

Published in the United States by
Firefly Books (U.S.) Inc.
P.O. Box 1338, Ellicott Station
Buffalo, New York 14205

Published in Canada by
Firefly Books Ltd.
66 Leek Crescent
Richmond Hill, Ontario L4B 1H1

Photographs: Harry Gils
Cover and interior design: Jeff Middleton
Page Production: Tinge Design Studio
Illustration: Dan Brandon

Printed in China

The publisher gratefully acknowledges the financial support for
our publishing program by the Government of Canada through
the Book Publishing Industry Development Program.

Dedication
For Bubs, and the eternal search for the Quick.

*The riders pictured in these pages are
experienced and are riding without protective
gear at their own risk. Like all sports, proper
protective gear should be worn at all times.
The publisher assumes no responsibility for
any injuries incurred as a result of trying the
tricks and techniques in this book.*

Contents

Introduction

I am by no means the best skateboarder in the world. In fact, I'm probably among the worst in the world. People who know me will probably laugh themselves stupid when they hear I wrote a book containing skateboarding instruction.

But hey, just because you're a pro at something doesn't necessarily mean you can teach it. Imparting instruction isn't about doing, thankfully; it is about getting the right information and explaining it *simply enough that people can figure it out for themselves.*

And since I'm nowhere near being a professional skateboarder, I hit up my friends when putting this book together. A lot of them. I consulted skateboarders of every stripe and skill level I could — and each lent their expertise to this thing. The end result is the culmination of a lot of experiences, not just mine.

That said, I think you'll find that these skateboarding instructions are the most straightforward out there, bar none. Trust me, I checked.

Now, there's hundreds upon hundreds of tricks and variations of tricks in skateboarding, so there's no way I could possibly cram every single one into this book — I'd need waaaay more space than I've got here, believe me. So this guide is a primer of sorts — the basic tricks to give you a foundation to build on.

Instruction aside, I also wanted to give you a taste of what skateboarding's really about — not just the mechanics of it, but what the subculture is about.

I'm going to give you an overview of the skate world (its history, industry, etc) so you don't spend your first year saying dumb things and annoying those around you. Consider this book as you would your big brother — someone who's going to make sure you're off to a good start and not totally embarrassing yourself.

Why? Because skateboarders look out for one another — you'll learn that lesson pretty quick — there's something about skating that binds people together once they've spent a couple years pushing themselves around on a piece of wood. It's like a fraternity, but without the stupid sweaters and secret handshakes.

In 10 years, maybe you won't skate anymore. But one thing is for certain, once a skateboarder, always a skateboarder.

Ryan Stutt

Skateboarding 101

Hard Goods

HOW EACH PIECE OF YOUR SKATEBOARD IS PUT TOGETHER, AND HOW THEY WORK.

There's nothing more important to skateboarding than a skateboard. By "skateboard" I mean the six different parts that comprise it: skate deck, wheels, trucks, bearings, bolts and grip tape.

You can buy a complete setup, which comes preassembled, but they're usually cheap, and you'll have to replace them sooner than you think. If there's one constant in skateboarding, it's that your setup will have the crap beaten out of it on a daily basis. Parts break from stress, crack from impacts and need to be replaced. Saving a little money up front may sound like a good idea, but you'll soon be suffering from buyer's remorse.

My advice? Buy the parts separately and spend a little extra money on quality stuff. The components won't all last forever, but some, such as your trucks, will definitely last longer and work better if they're higher quality. It's also a lot cheaper to buy a new deck or set of wheels every now and then rather then a whole new setup every month.

You may not particularly care about this wear and tear now, but it's important you know how your skateboard works mechanically. Why? Because you're the one who's going to be repairing and replacing the stuff.

SKATE DECKS

The graphics may vary, but every skate deck is made of seven layers of Canadian maple of the same size and shape. They are coated with resin glue and held under pressure until the resin dries and the plies are stuck together. The piece of wood at the bottom of the pile is called the bottom sheet, which is where the graphics are painted. The one you stand on is called the top sheet.

The pieces of maple are shaped with a tail and a nose. The angle of the nose is slightly less sharp than that of the tail, but both curve upward. The board also curves from the toe side to the heel side, called the concave. This concave shape strengthens the board's design and gives the rider better control of the board.

Your regularly accepted street skating board can vary in size from 7 to $8^1/_4$ inches (17.75 to 21 cm) wide, with proportional length. Anything above or below those sizes is an anomaly these days. Most people ride boards under 8 inches (20.25 cm) wide.

THE SMALLER THE RIDER, THE SMALLER THE BOARD?

Height is the best rule to follow when first buying a deck. You can buy kids' decks that are smaller than the average 7-inch (17.75 cm) skateboard width, and if your are under 4 feet (1.2 m) tall, a smaller deck is probably not a bad idea. Over 4 feet tall, a 7-inch deck is about the right size. But, that said, whatever you're more comfortable with is the best choice.

The concave also varies from board to board. The best way to know which angle you prefer is to actually skate it, but standing on one at a skate shop should give you an idea of how it feels.

Most decks will only last you a month or two, tops, especially if you skate them every day. This is hard on parents, since it gets expensive to buy a new deck every 30 to 60 days, but that's the reality of skateboarding.

While some companies have gimmicky technology they claim makes their boards last longer — usually it involves adding a sheet of fiberglass, bamboo, plastic or carbon fiber to the seven plies of wood — it doesn't usually do much. The extra sheet probably helps, but if your skateboard is getting a lot of use, it will break no matter what's inside it.

SKATEBOARD ART

Talking about skate art isn't easy to do. It's an incredibly important element of skateboarding, but when you try to put what it means to skateboarding into words, it almost always sounds stupid — a beret-wearing-art-snob kind of stupid.

There's been tens of thousands of deck graphics produced since skateboarding's infancy, ranging from shocking to insightful, from gross to hilarious and from really good to just plain stupid. But they were all (and continue to be) part of what makes skateboarding what it is. Each generation of graphics is different, but they're all very much the same — memorable.

There are hundreds of well-respected underground artists who got their start with skateboard graphics. Each contributed something iconic to skateboarding and helped make it what it is today.

Some important advice for the first-time skateboard buyer: you'll always remember the graphic on the first deck you rode. Get what you are stoked on. Money is no object when it comes to this.

NOTE If you're interested in skate art, check out Sean Cliver's book *Disposable: A History of Skateboard Art*. It's a great look at the progression of skate graphics through the years.

WHEELS

There's not much to wheels' construction. They're round, they're made in a mold filled with polyurethane and they've got a hole in the middle of them.

Currently, the normal street skating wheel sizes are between 48 and 55 mm ($1^7/_8$–$2^1/_8$ inches), though most people tend to prefer 50-52 mm ($1^{15}/_{16}$–$2^1/_{16}$ inches).

A durometer measures the hardness of the wheels, indicated by something called the "A" rating. Hard wheels, closer to 100A, are better for speed, but they give you a rough ride on concrete. However, in a skate park or ramp, you're stoked. Soft wheels, lower than 90A, are good for comfort because they absorb more of the bumps on the road. Unfortunately, they're also slower.

Most wheels have a tread of straight lines that runs around the circumference. The tread doesn't serve much purpose, aside from when you're skating ramps, where it gives you a bit of traction and prevents you from slipping on the ramp's smooth surface.

Quality wheels retain their shape and don't get flat spots from too much wear. There's no magic formula to get good wheels — just buy recognizable brand named ones. Ask your local skate shop which ones they recommend. The prices on wheels vary, but not by much. Don't cheap out on wheels, as they're the first thing to go on a skateboard. Quality definitely matters when it's something you're rolling on.

TRUCKS

Arguably the most important part of the skateboard, trucks give you the ability to turn and control your skateboard while you roll. Trucks are made of aluminum and have two main parts. First is the baseplate, which is the part with holes that attaches to the board. What hangs from it is, oddly enough, called the hanger. Running through the hanger from left to right is the axle. That's the part to which you'll later attach the wheels.

Coming up from the baseplate and through the hole in the hanger is the kingpin. The kingpin (which is just a big bolt) keeps all these parts together, so if you tighten or loosen the kingpin you restrict or loosen the truck's mobility.

Between the kingpin and the baseplate and hanger are bushings. Bushings are little rubber circles that cushion the truck when it turns, so you don't have the constant creaking of metal every time you turn.

Much like wheels and boards, trucks vary in size and shape to match the rest of your gear. What size truck you ride depends on your board. Ask at your skate shop to make sure you've got the right size.

The height of trucks also varies. You'll see low, mid and high trucks. A lot of factors come into play, but the type of truck you ride basically depends on what you're going to do with it. Low and mid trucks are better for street skating and flip tricks. Higher trucks allow you to ride bigger wheels, so they're better for vert and ramp skating.

I don't advocate specific brands anywhere else in this book, but when it comes to trucks, some are definitely better than others. The no-name brands tend to be cheap, in both senses of the word, but big brand companies also put out shoddy products. (I've even heard that some pros don't actually ride their sponsor's trucks.) Brands such as Independent, Venture and Thunder are consistently good.

You don't want to cheap out on trucks because they're the key to everything done on a skateboard. Plus, they're the most durable thing on your setup. A good set of trucks can last you all year. A cheap set could go in a matter of weeks.

BEARINGS

If you look at a skateboard wheel, you'll notice that the hole in the middle is surrounded by a wider, shallower hole. This is where the bearings go. Bearings are the little round balls inside your wheels that allow them to roll. If you look at how an axle fits through a set of bearing-set wheels, you'll notice that the axle never touches the wheel itself. It rests on the bearing, which in turn rests on the wheel.

It's the little ball bearings inside the bearing that move you along, not the wheels themselves. Without bearings, you might as well have square wheels.

You'll see the speed rating, called ABEC, on the packaging, but it doesn't matter to you. ABEC is a weird industrial rating that doesn't actually tell you how fast the bearings are for skateboarding. The reality is that bearings are pretty standard, and they all pretty much operate at the same speed.

That said, the "Swiss" bearings are, with reason, popular — they have a small design change that makes them last longer and provides a smoother, faster ride. But, there's always a "but," they cost a lot more. Are they worth it? Probably, but you don't need them to skate around,

and at a beginner's level you probably won't notice the difference. A mid-priced bearing should do you just fine.

NOTE There are two things you should never do to bearings: oil them or get them wet. Both will kill them pretty quickly.

GRIP TAPE

Grip tape is just black sandpaper with glue on the non-textured side. The rubber on the sole of your shoes "grips" the rough surface of the tape, giving you more control of your board than you would otherwise have. If you were skateboarding without grip tape, an ollie would be nearly impossible to do. You'd have no traction on your board, and you'd likely lose control pretty quickly. One sheet of grip isn't much better than another.

BOLTS

Just screws and nuts, kids. If someone tells you it's something more, they're lying. No bolt is going to make you a better skater. Bolts just keep your trucks attached to your deck, holding your skateboard together. Get whatever ones you like, as they're pretty much all the same.

Soft Goods

JUST AS IMPORTANT AS YOUR SETUP.

SHOES

Skateboarding is hard on shoes. It's not a surprise, really, when you consider that grip tape is like coarse sandpaper and skateboarding involves rubbing your shoes all over that sandpaper.

There's a ton of different styles of skate footwear — high tops, low tops, mid tops, made from hemp, leather, suede materials, with tons of different soles. Some don't even look like sneakers. The one thing they all have in common is that they were built with skateboarding in mind.

Regular sneakers, while fine for skateboarding, get chewed up pretty quickly. Most skate shoe companies have, smartly, designed their shoes specifically for skateboarding, meaning that areas that see a lot of wear and tear, such as the outside edge of your front toe, which is used to ollie, are reinforced. They also give you more ankle support and heel cushioning, since those are the areas where skateboarders need a little extra help.

I can't vouch for every skate shoe out there, but they generally last longer than regular sneakers. Not to say they're indestructible, because they're not, but they'll hang in there for longer than your average cross trainer.

Are they worth the extra money? I'd say they are, but you'll need to convince your mom. You can try to tell her that skate shoes aren't much more than the average sneaker these days.

THINGS TO LOOK FOR IN A SKATE SHOE

Ankle support More padding and structured support around the ankle helps to avoid sprains. It's not a guarantee, but it should help keep you from rolling your ankle.

Sturdy construction Not every skate shoe is going to be built like a tank but, as with any shoe, a quick inspection will tell you how well it's built. Check seams, the heel, the ankle — if it feels cheap, you don't want to skate in it.

Heel support In skateboarding, you take a lot of impacts to your heels, probably due the amount of jumping up and down. As such, look for good heel cushion in your shoe.

Covered seams Around the toe and sides of your average shoe are seams, where the material is sewn together. These areas wear while skateboarding, so look for covered seams, which are more durable.

A good sole There are a couple of different sole styles out there, but they are all made of gum rubber. You should look for one with an equal amount of support and "feel," meaning there is sufficient padding to protect you from impacts, but not so much padding you can't feel the board beneath your feet.

Breathability Your feet are going to sweat (a lot) while skateboarding. Without little vents in the design, your feet are going to stink something awful.

CLOTHING

Comfortable clothing that's not restrictive is all you need to skateboard. You don't need to wear "skate" brand-name clothing. At all. (There's no magic shirt that's going to help you kick flip better.) It comes down to fashion. Some skaters like baggy hip-hop style clothing, some like tight-fitting rock-and-roll style garb, the rest of us just wear what's comfortable.

That said, skate companies do make their products a little more skate friendly, with features such as reinforced seams and crotches and pants in flexible fabric, such as spandex, all of which are design considerations meant to improve clothing performance and durability. Overall, the clothes will not make the man (or woman) in this instance.

If there's a reason to buy the stuff, it's to look cool and, more importantly, to support the brands that give back to skateboarding — the companies that sponsor riders, put out videos, advertise in magazines and keep skateboarding going.

THINGS TO LOOK FOR IN PANTS

Reinforced seams Double stitching in areas that see a lot of wear and stress, such as the crotch, makes them last a lot longer in some cases.

Flexible fabrics Some pants have a flexible spandex-type material added in with the cotton or denim to give it some extra, well, give. It makes them easier to move in so you can avoid tears and breaks.

Breathable fabrics Same principle as the shoes. You work up a sweat while skating, and anything that helps you cool down is a plus. If an article of clothing helps you release all that heat better, it's a good thing.

SAFETY GEAR

Here's a very unpopular view among skateboarders, which I'll share with you anyway: you need to wear safety gear when learning how to skate. Yes, you might not look cool, but you won't look very cool laid up in a hospital bed covered in drool with a head injury, and the busted elbow that you get learning how to ollie isn't going to do wonders for your reputation either.

Wearing safety gear is no guarantee against injury, but it's going to help.

HELMETS

At the very least, a helmet should be worn while learning to skate. There are tons of companies putting them out in every size and color, and many styles don't look too bad (better than bike helmets anyway).

Your helmet should be snug fitting but not painful when on your head. If it slides around when you move, it's not tight enough. Only buy a helmet approved by a safety standards organization, such as the U.S. Consumer Product Safety Commission or the Canadian Standards Association, otherwise it may not be good enough to protect your noggin from harm.

KNEE AND ELBOW PADS

Definitely a must (along with a helmet) for kids learning transition skating. Pads should be tight, but not so tight that they restrict mobility (or blood flow). If your limbs go numb, loosen them up a bit. There are multisport knee and elbow pads (particularly BMX pads) that'll work for skateboarding.

WRIST GUARDS

Wrist guards are gloves with a reinforced plastic or metal bar along the wrist and palm that protect against wrist injuries. They're generally not used for skateboarding, but, if you're comfortable wearing something a Rollerblader would wear, you'll have extra peace of mind.

Putting Your Board Together

**HERE'S HOW TO PUT YOUR BOARD
TOGETHER IN 22 EASY STEPS
(BUT, SERIOUSLY, IT'S EASY).**

PART 1: BOARD AND GRIP

Putting grip on can be a pain in the butt.
The easiest way is to lay the board flat
across your lap with the top sheet (the
side with the ends bent towardsyou) up.

You'll need your board, grip tape, a file, a
utility knife and an Allen wrench (Allen
key) or bolt.

1. Take the wax paper off the bottom of
the grip tape.

2. Next, place the grip sticky side
down on the nose and tail with an even
surplus at either end and each side
of the board. Once you're sure you've
covered the entire top sheet evenly,
push down on one end of the grip to
attach it.

3. Then lay your hand out as flat as
you can and slowly push the grip tape
evenly down on the board. There's no
need to rush — you need to be sure
there are no air bubbles trapped under
the grip. Work your way back to the
other end of the board. Again, watch for
air bubbles and that the grip is evenly
covering the board.

PART 2: BOARD MEETS TRUCKS, THANKS TO BOLTS

Once your board is covered in grip and the eight holes are punched, you'll need your hardware — eight bolts and eight nuts — and an Allen wrench (Allen key) and wrench (or skate tool, as pictured).

4. Now that you've got the grip on, take the file and rub it on the edges of your board. It makes an outline that you'll use to cut off the excess grip so it's not crooked.

5. Now it's chopping time. Assuming you're old enough to use a knife, push it in through the sticky side of the grip, near the edge of the board. Make sure it's at a sharp angle. Slide the knife along the board, cutting along the outline you created. If cut right, the grip should cover only the top sheet and not hang over the sides of the other sheets.

6. If you did a lousy job, smooth off the edges with a bit of excess grip.

7. Finally, poke eight holes in the grip with an Allen wrench or bolt so you can fit your hardware through it.

1. Starting at one end, put four bolts through the holes in the top of your board.

2. Next, use one hand to keep the bolts pushed in all the way and turn your board upside down so you can see the bolts sticking out of the bottom. Put one set of trucks on the bolts with the kingpin facing toward the center of the board.

3. Still holding the bolts with your hand push the truck flush with the bottom of the board. On the other side, the heads of the bolts should now be flush with the top of the board.

4. Thread the bolts onto the screws as right as you can with your hands.

5. Once all four screws are on, grab a wrench or skate tool and an Allen wrench. Hold the screw in place with the Allen wrench and tighten the bolts with the wrench or skate tool until the top of the bolt is flush with, or embedded in, the grip, and the nut is as tight as you can make it. Repeat with the other three bolts.

6. Repeat steps one to four on the other truck.

PART 3: WHEELS AND BEARINGS

First off, take a look at the wheels. You'll note there is a little indentation around the hole in the middle, with a smaller hole in the middle. The indent is where the bearings go. Getting them on is a bit hard, but here's the easiest way:

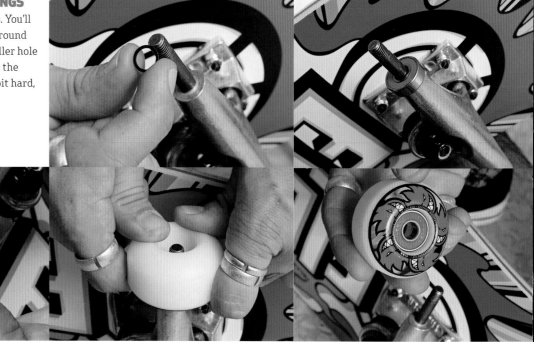

1. Take the nut and washer off the end of one of the axels. Put them somewhere you won't lose or forget about them.

2. Next, toss a bearing on the axle.

3. Grab a wheel and put it on the axle on top of the bearing.

4. With the board on the ground, push down on the wheel until you feel the

bearing go into the hollowed-out portion of the wheel as far as it can go.

5. Voila. The bearing is set in the wheel. Repeat this on the other side of the wheel and for all the other wheels.

PART 4: TRUCKS, WHEELS AND BEARINGS

You've got the wheels and bearings put together, so now you need to put them onto the board and trucks.

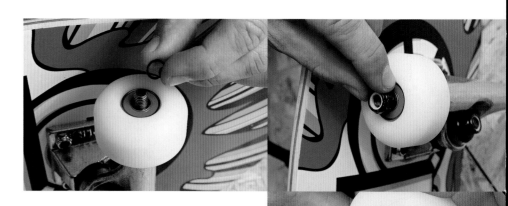

1. Take the bolt off the end of the axle and remove one of the two washers. Keep it in a safe place. Take a wheel (art facing in or out, it doesn't matter) and place it on the axle. The one washer that you didn't remove should now sit between the axle and the wheel.

2. Once the wheel is on, put the other washer on the axle and put the bolt back on.

3. Tighten the bolt until the wheel doesn't move from side to side. Repeat for all four wheels.

PART 5: MAKE SURE EVERYTHING IS PERFECT

Now use a wrench or skate tool to adjust the trucks as loose or tight as you like. If you find your grip job is a little uneven, take a scrap piece of grip and sand the edges down until everything looks perfect.

That's it. Congratulations, you've just put together a skateboard.

The Evolution of Four Wheels on Wood

IT'S COME AND GONE, BUT SKATEBOARDING HAS BEEN AROUND FOR OVER 50 YEARS.

The styles have changed drastically over the years—from a fad born on the beach by surfers looking for something to do in between tides in the 50s and 60s to the activity of choice among social outcasts in the late 80s and early 90s. If you took a skater from the 60s and a skater from the 90s and put them side by side without boards, you'd never know they were into the same sport.

Skateboards themselves have also changed since their inception and continue to evolve today. Will we ever see a hoverboard like Michael J. Fox rode in *Back to the Future*? Probably not, but there was also a time when no one thought flipping your board was possible, so who knows?

THE 50s AND 60s

Skateboarding was born out of surfing — it's the bastard child of wave riding. While we don't know who invented the skateboard, most agree skateboarding originates with scooters kids used to ride. Some kids ripped the scooter's handle out of the board and just pushed around without it.

However, they couldn't turn. In the late 50s, a surfer got the bright idea to tweak the design by putting roller skate trucks and wheels on the bottom of a mini surfboard. The skateboard became an alternative for surfers who wanted to ride waves when there were no waves to be had.

These were the days of freestyle riding and, looking back, it looks pretty funny when you compare it to the skateboarding of today. During these early years, skateboarding got pretty popular. The first skateboard magazine, *Skateboarder*, was started, and tens of millions of boards were sold by companies such as Hobie Skateboards.

But by the mid- to late 60s, the shine had worn off skateboarding, and it was dismissed as just another fad. *Skateboarder* went belly up, and the skateboard itself went the way of the hula-hoop for about 10 years.

The boards These early years were the era of the "banana board." These boards had a very slim width, only around 6 to 7 inches (15 to 18 cm) on average. With no bent nose or tail, they were just a flat, narrow piece of wood or fiberglass with lousy clay wheels and roller skate trucks attached.

THE 70s

When skateboarding was popular in the 60s, it suffered from one horrible handicap above all others: clay wheels. They were loud, hard to ride on, slippery and probably what killed skateboarding's first incarnation. Thankfully, the 70s saw a huge leap forward in skateboard design and technology.

In the early 70s, Frank Nasworthy developed a skateboard wheel made out of polyurethane, which provided a super smooth ride. Then, in 1975, a company called Road Rider introduced the first precision skateboard bearing, which helped skaters achieve more consistent speeds. The cherry on top was placed around 1976, when skate trucks were redesigned by a company called Tracker Trucks, who made them turn easier and more consistently.

Suddenly skateboards were a lot more fun to ride, and skaters had a lot more control of their boards. The possibilities of what you could do on a board started to open up.

By the end of 1976, skateboarding resurged, thanks in no small part to the Z-Boys (Tony Alva, Stacy Peralta and Jay Adams), who turned freestyle skating into something a little more innovative. Pools were skated, grabs were done and progressive skateboarding was born.

It was also during this period that Alan "Ollie" Gelfand invented the ollie, which would be the basis for a huge push forward in the progression of skateboarding, though few realized it at the time.

However, as far as the mainstream was concerned, skateboarding was still a fad. BMX was the new king, and as if to make sure skateboarding was really dead, *Skateboarder* (which had resurfaced once skateboarding got popular again) turned into BMX-centric *Action Now* magazine. Skateboarding died off (again) and went underground.

The boards Skateboards got a tail, thanks to Larry Stevenson, and got wider (becoming around 9 inches/23 cm wide), but they were still flat, with little to no concave. Technology was improving though, with better bearings, wheels and trucks. It was also the era where graphics were introduced to the bottom of boards.

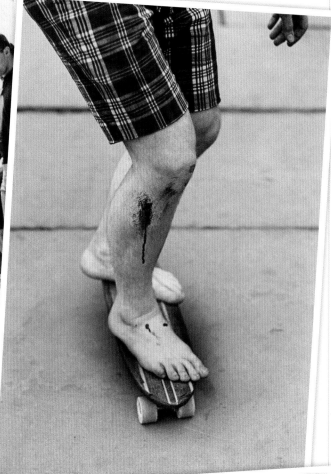

Above Left: Students at Wesleyan University watch a skateboarder carve through a slalom course.

Above Right: A skater shows off his cut leg while riding barefoot on a banana board.

Bottom: A skater carves in an early skate park in 1977.

Top: Christian Hosoi competes at the Skateboarding World Championships at Expo 1986 in Vancouver, Canada.

Above: Sean Malto competing during "Slaughter at the Opera" at the Sydney Opera House in Sydney, Australia, March 1, 2008.

Right: An 18-year-old Tony Hawk taking a break from practice in 1986.

THE 80s

This era of skateboarding was dominated by three skate companies: Powell Peralta, Vision/Sims and Santa Cruz. They had the best teams and the coolest boards. It was also a decade of new starts for skate media. *Thrasher* magazine started publishing in 1981, and *TransWorld Skateboarding* started up in 1983. The first ever skate video, *The Bones Brigade Video Show*, was released in 1985 by Powell-Peralta.

There was no question, as far as mainstream popularity was concerned, that vert was king for most of the 80s. Guys such as Tony Hawk, Christian Hosoi, Lance Mountain and Neil Blender toured the world blowing minds with what they could do on a ramp.

But street skating, which is the more popular form of skateboarding today, also progressed. Tommy Guerrero, Mark Gonzales, Rodney Mullen and Natas Kaupas were doing things no one had thought possible on rails, ledges and streets.

Professional skateboarders were making real money doing what they loved thanks to contest winnings and board royalties. It would lead to a whole new reality for the skateboard industry that no one would see coming.

No, skateboarding didn't die again, it did get turned on its head though. (But in a good way.)

The boards Boards got a lot wider during the 80s and companies introduced a slew of (needless) "improvements" to skateboards: plastic tail guards, nose guards, lappers, coppers and rails were introduced, but none would stay attached to boards past 1989.

THE 90s

This decade was a turning point for skateboarding. In the late 80s, in response to the big three companies essentially owning skateboarding, former Sims pro skater Steve Rocco started a little company called World Industries and, later, Blind Skateboards.

With legendary skaters such as Jason Lee, Mike Vallely, Natas Kaupas and Mark Gonzales on board, World Industries started the new trend of skater owned and operated companies. More importantly, these riders revolutionized what people thought could be done on a skateboard. It was an instant hit with kids.

Well, some kids. Skateboarding wasn't in the public eye any longer — it had gone underground. Those who loved it, loved it, but they were social outcasts compared to the skaters of today. Back then you were more likely to get beaten up for being a skateboarder, rather than getting girls and your own reality show.

Graphics were controversial. They didn't just push the boundaries of good taste, they stomped all over them. Rocco started *Big Brother* magazine in 1992, which drove parents across the country so crazy on so many levels that it deserves its own book.

It was the start of a groundbreaking era of skateboarding: street skating. Street skating reigned supreme, and vert skating took a backseat due to a lack of facilities. It was a lot easier for kids to just roll around their neighborhood and skate.

It was also a new era for skate videos, with Blind's *Video Days*, Plan B's *Questionable*, Toy Machine's *Welcome to Hell* and Zero's *The Thrill of it All* pushing the limits of street skating. Any kid with access to a VCR could get a new video and apply what he or she saw to local skate spots. The skateboard world got a little smaller. Suddenly, anything was skateable.

By the end of the 90s, skateboarding exploded in popularity with mainstream television coverage in ESPN's X-Games. It hasn't looked back since.

The boards "Big pants, small wheels" was the order of the day. Boards themselves got narrower, settling in at the 7- to 8-inch (18 to 20 cm) widths we commonly see today, with a nose and tail and concaves in the boards.

TODAY

Skateboarding is here to stay. Its popularity has waned a bit, but there's no imminent crash coming. It's as big as baseball or soccer in terms of participation. There are thousands of people around the world who skateboard for a living in one way or another.

Skateboarders are treated like athletes, not hobbyists. They have reality TV shows, present at award shows and probably earn more money than your average astronaut. There are more skate magazines than ever and more quality skate parks than anyone could have ever imagined.

Skateboarding's crossed the barrier from fad into established sport. There's a very real likelihood of skateboarding being in the Olympics in the very near future. (If that's not mainstream acceptance, I don't know what is.)

The boards Today you're lucky to be riding the pinnacle of board, wheel, truck and bearing design. Skateboards have never had as much research and development put into them as they do today. They're lighter, stronger and, arguably, more durable.

Skate Media Primer

MAGAZINES

There's been nothing more important to skateboard culture than the skate magazine. From day one they've been the historians of skateboarding — the record keepers, the trendsetters, the people helping to evolve skateboarding by showcasing what's happening on the streets of the world every month. It's hard to imagine what skateboarding would be like today without the influence of the skate magazine.

The good news is you won't have to search that hard to find a skate magazine. Currently, there's a ton of them out there, available everywhere from corner stores to skate shops to newsstands.

In the United States alone, there are five big magazines: *Transworld Skateboarding*, *Thrasher*, *The Skateboard Mag*, *Slap* and *Skateboarder*. There are also a ton more, such as *SBC* in Canada and *Kingpin* and *Document* in Europe.

Each is great in its own way, but some you'll like more than others — it depends on your sensibilities. One thing they all share is amazing photography and giving you a chance to witness the monthly evolution of skateboarding.

Every pro and am skater in the world remembers the first photo he or she got in a skate magazine. It's a defining moment that not a lot of skateboarders get to have in their lives. If you're lucky, maybe it'll happen to you too. For now though, just enjoy the read.

VIDEOS

A skateboarding video is a compilation of clips of skateboarders doing various tricks and lines set to music. There may be skits and arty stuff in between, but the gist of it is the skateboarding. Sometimes they're done by an individual director, sometimes they're put together by a skate magazine and sometimes they're done by companies to help promote their products by promoting their team of riders.

Skate videos are one of the most fun things about skateboarding, even though they aren't actually skateboarding. Much like magazines, skate videos are record keepers of skateboarding, but in a slightly different way. You get the same great feats, the name making, the mind blowing, the new spots, the evolution, but you get to see it happen in real time.

You see how sketchy that takeoff and landing really were. What an idiot that security guard was. How everyone watching lost their minds when a rider landed the trick everyone thought was impossible. Videos are a pretty rad thing.

They give you a chance to witness the evolution of skateboarding and inspiration to go out there and tear some spots up yourself. Nothing gets you quite so stoked to go out and skate as watching a really good video. (Consider it a "pregame" ritual, if you want to get all into sports analogies.)

Now the bad news. It used to be that when a company released a skate video you'd wear through the VHS copy of it from overuse. Now, with DVDs and the Internet, you can watch them over and over again in perfect quality, and you can get them for free. Unfortunately, the filmmakers, editors and skaters who work so hard to put together a banging video don't get paid when it's downloaded for free, which makes it harder for more videos to be put out. So do us all a favor and resist the urge to download, okay?

RECOMMENDED VIEWING

You may have to hunt for some of these, but here's a short list of some of the most recommended, must-see videos around. This isn't some top-10 list, just a few that came to mind that will probably set you in the right direction…

Hokus Pokus (H-Street Skateboards, 1989)
Video Days (Blind Skateboards, 1991)
Questionable (Plan B Skateboards, 1992)
20 Shot Sequence (World Industries, 1995)
Mouse (Girl Skateboards, 1996)
Welcome to Hell (Toy Machine Skateboards, 1996)
Menikmati (éS footwear, 2000)
The DC Video (DC Shoes, 2003)
Yeah Right! (Girl Skateboards, 2003)
Lost and Found (Blueprint Skateboards, 2005)
Bag of Suck (Enjoi Skateboards, 2006)
What If? (Blind Skateboards, 2006)
This Is My Element (Element Skateboards, 2007)

Skate Documentation Primer

If there isn't proof, it didn't happen. That's the philosophy of a lot of skateboarders, so you'd better have some evidence your trick went down. These guides aren't going to make you a pro-level camera operator, but they will help you document your bud's moves better.

So, here's our resident skate photographer, Harry Gils, with a couple of documentation pointers.

PHOTOGRAPHY

1. Two types of shots The most basic skateboarding shots are the still and the sequence. A still is just that, one shot that captures the most important part of a trick. A sequence, on the other hand, is anywhere from three to 20 shots taken rapidly while someone is doing a trick so you capture the full range of what the skater is doing.

2. Lighting Ideally, most skate photographers have two to five or more flashes set up when they're shooting. You're unlikely to spend that kind of dough on flashes and stands unless you're super serious about skate photography. However, available light works great for some situations. Sometimes simple is better.

3. Sequences and frame rates Everything in skateboarding happens quickly, so it's important to have a camera with a high frame rate when shooting a sequence. Make sure that you have a camera capable of capturing at least seven or eight frames per second if you want good sequences.

4. Composition In any skate photo, you want a clear picture of what the subject is doing. That means the take off, landing and subject are in frame, and you're not accidentally cropping out an arm or part of the head. Learn the basics of general photography, such as the Rule of Thirds.

5. Background Not every photo you take is going to have a nice background. If you're shooting at a skate park you won't have much control of the background, but if you're shooting street skating, try to set your shot up so there's something interesting in the background or, more importantly, something that will make your skater pop out, such as the sky. Watch out for light posts or other objects that might look as though they're sticking out of the skater's head.

6. The gear You want to start out with a single lens reflex (SLR) camera. Point-and-shoot cameras don't have the high shutter speed or flash sync needed to shoot skateboarding. You need a 35mm manual film or digital SLR.

7. Digital vs film There was a time when fledgling photographers would spend hundreds of dollars on film while experimenting and learning how to shoot. With a digital camera you can save a pile of money and get instant feedback on your photography. You can also get a used film camera for cheap, but remember, film still costs a butt load.

8. Lenses Most skateboard photographers use two lenses, a fish-eye and a telephoto or zoom lens.

9. Save some money Get it used. There's no sense paying full price for a new camera and gear. Hit used camera stores and Internet sites like eBay to find better deals. Just because it's used doesn't mean it won't work for you.

10. Stopping the action Skateboarding is a fast activity, so having a fast shutter speed is essential. Plan on at least 1/1000 of a second if you are shooting available light, or 1/250 of a second flash sync if you are using flashes during the day.

FILM

There's nothing quite like the satisfaction of landing a trick you've been trying for hours and being able to watch it 10 seconds later on your friend's camcorder. But filming isn't as easy as it looks. Like skateboard photography, there are tricks that make it better and easier.

1. The right camera At the very least you're going to need a digital video (DV) camera. That's not to say you can't use a film camcorder, but the footage is harder to edit. With DV cameras, you can dump your footy onto a computer and have a clip edited in minutes.

2. Lenses The lens on your camcorder is probably poor for filming skateboarding. You can use it, but you should get an adapter and attach a fish-eye or wide-angle lens to what you've got (chances are the lens isn't removable). Any camera store should be able to set you up.

3. Filming lines You film a line by skating behind someone and filming them as they roll along and land a bunch of tricks one after another. The secret here is to get all the tricks on tape by staying close enough to get all the action, but not so close that you can't tell what's going on. Same goes for being too far behind them — the last thing you want to watch is some blurry dot doing something that looks similar to skateboarding. You need to give the audience some perspective of what's going on.

Above: This photograph of a cameraman properly filming a line illustrates good use of the Rule of Thirds. Dividing a photograph into thirds, both horizontally and vertically, creates a grid of nine equal parts. By placing elements in the photograph along the lines and intersecting points of this grid, a photographer can create stronger, more dynamic compositions.

4. Filming tricks Filming a stationary trick is pretty easy. Set up in an area that gives you a good angle on the action, meaning you have a full view of the takeoff and landing and you're not going to accidentally crop out a body part. Once you've got that down, get creative. Practice zooming and panning before and after a trick. Is there something interesting around the spot? Try to incorporate it into the shot. Another good piece of advice comes from a filmmaker friend of mine, Tomas Morrison, "I like to break clips down into three parts: an intro, the main trick and the outro. The intro and outro often contain panning and/or zooming."

5. Avoid gimmicky cameras Those stupid helmet cams are just that, stupid. They take stupid videos and make you look stupid when you wear them. If you're going to record yourself, use a real camcorder.

6. Editing You likely don't have access to professional-level video-editing programs, but there are tons of easy-to-use (and nearly free) programs out there that are good enough to make your video or clip look decent. Watch a lot of skate videos to get an idea of how you should edit yours together. Keep it tight. Cut out anything that isn't a roll up, trick, landing or roll away. (Your friends aren't that funny, trust me.)

7. The Internet is your friend With YouTube and other free video sites, you can post your footy up for the world to see, and then you can send the URL to your friends and family. However, don't e-mail companies with your links.

8. "Sponsor me" tapes You don't even want to think about sending potential sponsors tapes of yourself while you're still learning to skate. No one wants to watch you kick flip in your parent's driveway. Wait a couple years, and if you're blowing people's minds at the skate park then maybe think about putting a reel of yourself together.

Spots and Obstacles

**A GUIDE TO WHAT THE THINGS
YOU'RE SKATING ARE CALLED
AND WHAT YOU CAN DO ON THEM.**

1. BOWLS

Similar to a pool, but easier to skate. A bowl is a combination of a shallow round pool and a 360-degree mini-ramp.

2. HIPS

Hips are the side of a pyramid, where two inclined planes meet in the middle without a flat part between them, at anywhere from a 45- to 90-degree angle.

3. STAIR SETS

Exactly what it sounds like: a set of stairs you jump down. If there are two sets of stairs with a bit of flat between them, it's called a double set.

4. RAILS

Rails are handrails on staircases. You generally — once you're a good enough skater — do grind or slide tricks on them. Some are longer than others.

5. FLAT BARS

Much like a handrail, a flat bar is a long, square rail that's laid about a foot (30 cm) off the ground, which you can grind or slide on. It's usually found at skate parks.

6. WALLS

With a little bit of help, even walls are skateable, and doing so is called a wallride.

7. LEDGES

A ledge is normally made out of concrete, granite or, ideally, marble. You do grind or slide tricks on them.

8. HUBBAS

The fat ledge down the side of a set of stairs.

9. BENCHES

Pretty self-explanatory — they are benches you sit on or, in your case, do grinds or slides on.

10. BARRIERS

There are a couple of different types of barriers, such as plastic and concrete. Depending on the setup, you can grind, stall and slide on them.

11. MANNY PADS

A manny pad is a large rectangular surface that you ollie up on, perform manuals and hop off of. They vary in size and shape, but the use is the same.

12. LAUNCH RAMPS

Also called kickers. They were and still are a mainstay of suburban skating, when there are no skate parks or ramps to be had. It's a small ramp you skate up, which gives you a bit of air, so that you can do flip or grab tricks.

13. GAPS

A gap is the empty space between any two objects. They can be the same height, or one can be higher than the other.

14. PYRAMIDS

Mostly used at skate parks as obstacles, a pyramid is the same shape as the ones in Egypt, just at a less steep angle and with a flat top. You use them to get height to do flip or grab tricks in midair.

15. MINI-RAMPS

They vary in size, but all mini-ramps have the same characteristics: a flat bottom in the middle and transitions to coping on either side. You can do just about any trick on a mini.

16. QUARTER PIPES

Take a mini-ramp, cut it in four quarters and what you've got left is a quarter pipe. It is a transition leading from flat ground to a coping.

17. FULL PIPES

Full pipes are exactly what they sound like: completely rounded half pipes with no gaps in the surface other than the ends. You carve around in these.

18. HALF PIPES (AKA VERT RAMPS)

You're unlikely to ever skate one of these, but I thought I'd include them. Vert ramps are 10- to 16-foot (3–5 m) high mini-ramps with a lot more space between the transition and coping. There's a large straight-up-and-down vertical wall in this space (hence it's also called a vert). The same principles apply to both half pipes and mini-ramps; one is just way bigger than the other.

Skate Park Etiquette

HOW TO MAKE FRIENDS AND NOT ANNOY PEOPLE.

Nobody likes being "that guy" at the skate park; the one who skates into people, gets in their way, gets them hurt and is generally a pain in everyone's ass.

You might think that a skate park is some sort of all-you-can-skate buffet, and it is. While it won't ever replace street skating, there's something to be said for having access to nearly every type of obstacle you'd like to skate that day in one convenient location.

But here's the rub, you're not alone out there. There's a whole park full of skaters, and you all have to coexist peacefully (with the exception of Rollerblade and BMX guys, they don't count). For your safety and the safety of the people who have to skate with you, here's some things you should have in mind before you start pushing around in a skate park:

1. WATCH AND LEARN

Before you even think about getting out there, watch first. Pick the best skaters and watch them — what they do, where they go and how they interact with the other skaters. While you're not skating at their level, you can learn from how they go about their business at the park. If all else fails, try to be like those skaters.

2. OBSTACLES ARE NOT BENCHES

Don't sit on any obstacles. If you're just going to lurk and check stuff out, don't sit on something somebody might want to skate. Stick to the sidelines.

3. KEEP YOUR HEAD UP

When you're pushing around, so are other people. Be aware of what's going on around you and the lines people are skating. Running into other skaters is completely avoidable if you're not daydreaming about how awesome you might be some day.

4. DON'T TRY TO IMPRESS ANYONE

Pick a smart spot to learn tricks. Don't be embarrassed to learn how to skate on smaller stuff — that's what it's there for. You're going to get on people's nerves (not to mention hurt) if you try to learn boardslides on a rail you can't even ollie up on to while there's a line of skaters waiting to actually skate it.

5. WAIT YOUR TURN

A skate park is a lot like a playground. Everyone wants a turn riding the slide, and everyone wants to play on the monkey bars. Just like a playground, nobody likes a snake in line at the skate park. There's a pecking order to who skates first. Look around, make eye contact with the other people you're skating with and wait for the go-ahead.

Note While it varies, most skate parks in the United States make wearing a helmet mandatory for anyone skating at their facility. In some cases, they also make everyone wear full pads. Look into what the safety requirements are before you head to a skate park.

Skateboarding Hierarchy

IT'S NOT AS BAD AS IT SOUNDS.

If there's one constant among all skateboarders, it's the desire to get free gear. So it's no surprise that if skateboarding has a hierarchy — yes, even in something as antiauthoritarian as skateboarding there is a pecking order — it's partly determined by who gets the most free stuff.

It's not so much a class system, it's just how things work. You start at the bottom getting nothing for free and try to work your way up to where you get pretty much everything for free.

PROS

These are the guys (and girls) with signature boards, shoes, wheels, trucks, clothing — you name the product, they've got their name on it. By endorsing these products they get a bit of money for each product sold. They actually make a decent living off of skateboarding professionally and get to travel the world, living like nomadic rock stars.

Normally they'll have been at a professional level for two or three years before turning pro through the support of their sponsors.

AMS

Ams are below the pros. They're the younger guys and girls who are really good but haven't put the time in to be called pros. Once your name is on a board — it's called getting your pro model — you're considered a pro skateboarder. These skaters don't have their name on anything yet, but they might someday soon. These riders get pretty much everything for free, but they aren't getting royalty checks.

TEAMS

Pick any skate company, and it will have a roster of sponsored pro and am riders. The idea is to have a bunch of talented young riders and well-respected older pro riders associated with the company's brand. They tour to do demos and get footage for videos and magazines, which also promote the company.

FLOW RIDERS

They're kids from all over the world who are getting free stuff from skate companies. Why are they getting free stuff? Because someone from a skate company saw them skate and thought they had potential and would be a good person to represent the brand. They aren't getting paychecks, just free stuff and the odd free trip. It's still a pretty good deal.

SHOP RIDERS

Kids normally start out in skateboarding as shop riders — their local shop owner likes the way they skate and puts them on the shop team. They'll get some free decks and other gear when the shop feels like giving them stuff (and can afford to do so).

THE REST OF THE WORLD

The rest of us have to pay for everything. After all, someone's got to buy stuff so other people can make a living off of it. Take comfort in the fact that every time you buy a core skate product, your favorite riders are getting paid to skate.

You can only skate the same routes to the same spots for so long before you get supremely bored and want to knock yourself out with your own board. It's no wonder skateboarders hit the road as often as humanly (and financially) possible.

For pros and ams, traveling around the world is part of their lives. They pay the bills by getting footage for their sponsors and doing demos to promote their brands.

As for the rest of us? Not so much. We have to settle for a trip to a neighboring city or a skate park that's a little out of the way. Still, anything that's new is worth the trip.

So you and too many of your friends hop in a car and hit the road. As weird as it sounds, there's something about being locked in a van with a bunch of your smelly friends on your way to a whole new place to skate. Somebody's going to be the hero and land something big. Someone's going to bail right away and mope for the rest of the trip. Someone's going to be the "responsible one" for the trip. Someone's going to mouth off and get in trouble, which someone else will have to sort out.

It's all part of a skate road trip, and it's one of the most fun things about skateboarding.

Welcome to Skateboarding

TIPS AND WISDOM FOR KIDS, ADOLESCENTS AND ADULTS (AKA PARENTS).

CORE SKATE SHOPS

It may seem hard to believe, but that smelly tattooed guy at the core skate shop who looks like he just got out of prison is going to be your new best friend. The core skate shop (that is, the smaller, independently owned store rather than a chain) gives you something a mall store can't — loyalty. Core shop owners depend on your repeat business, so they are always going to treat you right.

A mall store will have lower prices on some stuff, but half the time they won't know what they're talking about. The

teenager working the counter isn't going to look out for you, or provide credible advice. A mall store probably won't encourage you to get better at skateboarding. They probably won't support you with a shop sponsorship. And they definitely wont brag about you to the skate companies they deal with, which might end up getting you sponsorships. An independently owned skate shop will do all of these things.

Try to resist the urge to save a couple of bucks by shopping at the mall store, and help give back to skateboarding by supporting the little guy that is at the heart of skateboarding in your community.

SPONSORSHIPS

Skate companies and shops like to sponsor kids who show potential. They'll give these kids free gear, which helps promote their brand and helps out the next generation of aspiring skateboarders.

That said, you aren't going to get sponsored anytime soon. Getting to

a talent level in skateboarding that companies are stoked on takes years to achieve — you don't need to go fishing for sponsorships or an agent just yet.

Keep your eyes and ears open, be active in your skate community and let your skills do the talking. If you are getting phone calls from tons of companies looking to hook you up, then you may want to talk to your parents about helping you manage your skateboarding career.

But getting free swag does not mean it is time to get a huge ego. This is the first step in the long line of becoming a professional skateboarder. And skateboarding, like any sport, is a relative long shot as a career. It is just as hard to become the next Tony Hawk, as it is to become the next Peyton Manning.

Just enjoy skateboarding and forget the whole "going pro" thing. If you have the talent, things will happen. If not, who cares? You can still skate and enjoy the free swag while you're doing the dental hygienist program at DeVry.

NOTE TO PARENTS

HELMETS AND PADS

No amount of padding can protect your kid from every possible injury. Skateboarding, like any other sport,

has its risks. However, safety gear is important – here are some tips:

Helmets As much as any kid is going to complain about it, make sure he or she

is wearing a helmet at all times when skating. A lot of skateboarders will tell you that helmets are lame and useless, but you — and your kid — should ignore them.

It may be a hard argument to win: no professional skateboarders in magazines or videos wear a helmet or pads unless they're skating a vert ramp. Also, most of the older kids your child will see skating around won't be wearing pads either. However, your kid isn't a professional or an experienced skater. Your child is jumping around on an unstable surface with wheels, and they are going to fall, on concrete. *Wear the helmet.*

Pads You're probably also going to have a hard time getting your kid to wear pads at all times. When he or she is first learning how to get around on a board, pads are a good idea. When starting out, your child will be falling a lot. Pads will save them a few skinned knees and bruises.

However, the pads can usually be set aside safely before the helmet can. Skateboarding isn't a contact sport, and your kid is unlikely to be skating anything large enough to warrant elbow pads, kneepads and wrist guards. Once he or she has learned how to take a fall, a helmet should be all your child needs.

SOCCER MOMS (OR DADS) NEED NOT APPLY

Kids don't want their parents hanging out at the skate park all day, and they don't want them cheering from the sidelines. Skateboarding isn't a team sport with a discernible start and finish. It's very relaxed and laid back — more about having fun than winning.

Supporting your kid is great, but skateboarding requires less of your involvement. You're not going to find a lot of parents getting into things on the sidelines at skate parks and skate spots. A good skate mom or dad will offer a lift and be content to hear about the session later.

SKATEBOARDING ISN'T INHERENTLY BAD.

There's a chance your kid will get in trouble through skateboarding. Even though it's on TV and used to sell everything from clothing to cars, the law enforcement community has been slow to embrace skateboarding. Internet chat rooms and news sites are abuzz with videos of police stopping kids skating.

Sometimes the skate park gets boring, and often, the best skate spots are located on or near sites where skateboarding is prohibited. While this isn't ideal, there are worse things your child could be doing. The consequences of a visit from the police with your son or daughter in tow is a personal matter, but when confronted with the issue try to remember that skateboarding is not a crime.

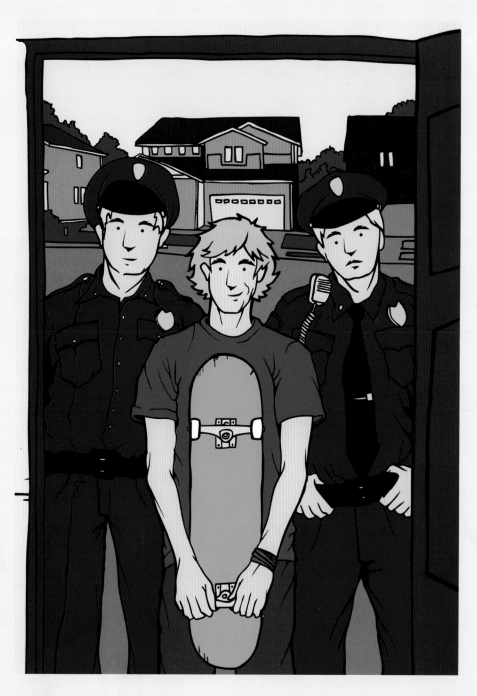

Flat Ground Basics

'CAUSE, YOU KNOW, IT HAPPENS ON THE FLAT PART OF THE GROUND. DUH.

Now that I've explained all the culture and history stuff, let's get down to the actual skateboarding. That's what you're here for, isn't it? You don't want to just read about skateboarding, you want to get on that board and shred.

While most of this chapter will sound pretty simple and straightforward, trust me, you're going to suck at most of these things for the time being. Actually, you're going to suck for a month or two, but don't feel bad. You're not weird, and you're not an uncoordinated simpleton. Skateboarding just takes time to learn. Everybody who skates started where you are now: standing on a skateboard looking like a newborn deer taking its first steps. Pushing around and hopping up curbs looks easy when you see an experienced skater do it, but getting on a board and doing it yourself is totally different. So here's where I start to get you comfortable with your skateboard.

This section explains the most basic parts of skating — all the little things you'll be doing so often that, eventually, you won't even notice you're doing them. They'll become second nature to you. Things like figuring out which way you ride (regular or goofy), hopping on your board, pushing yourself, stopping, turning and kicking your board up.

You'll also learn the difference between switch and fakie. Then we'll get to some basic tricks — ollies, nollies and, quite possibly the most fun trick you can do on the ground, the manual.

By the time you're through you'll have a pretty good grasp of skateboarding, or at least a pretty good idea of how the basics work. With practice — a lot of practice — you should be up and around on a skateboard in no time.

TERMS YOU SHOULD KNOW:

NOSE The slightly less concave end of your board, which is pointed in front of you.

TAIL The more concave end of your board, which is always facing away from you.

FRONT FOOT The foot that stays on your board while you push. Your front foot is, obviously, the foot that stays in front of you while you skate.

BACK FOOT Also known as your pushing foot, your back foot is … wait for it … normally always going to be placed behind you on your board.

Stance

ARE YOU A REGULAR RUNT? OR A GOOFY GROM?

The first thing you need to figure out is which way you're going to stand on your board as you ride — your "stance." It's dictated by which foot you lead with (the one in front of you, toward the nose) and which foot you push with (the foot behind you, near the tail).

A good way to figure out your stance, without ever actually stepping on a board, is to consider how you slide on ice or a wet floor. Whichever foot you naturally put out in front of you is likely to be your leading foot on a skateboard. If you feel more comfortable leading off with your left foot then you're regular. If you lead with your right foot then you, my friend, are goofy.

Neither is better or worse, it's just a comfort thing. People are naturally more comfortable balancing on one foot or the other. Don't worry, no one's going to make fun just because your stance is goofy. In this regard (unlike most situations) being goofy is pretty harmless.

SWITCH

Doing something "switch" (some people still refer to it as "switch stance," but these people are very, very old) means that instead of having your comfortable foot forward during a trick, you have your weak foot forward. So if you're normally facing right when you're standing on your board you face left. Vice versa if you're one of those goofy fellas.

Why is it such a big deal when you see things done switch in videos or magazines? Well, have you ever tried writing with your other hand? See how hard it is? Skateboarding with your wrong foot is the same. It completely throws you off.

Unless you're supremely ambidextrous, you're suddenly using the opposite set of muscles, which have been sitting around doing nothing. You lead with a particular foot for a reason: it feels more natural, comfortable

and balanced. All that comfort is gone when you ride switch.

Get used to riding switch now so you don't have to relearn everything as you progress. You might struggle more to learning everything, but you'll blow people's minds when they see how boss you are at riding switch.

FAKIE

In most other board sports, fakie and switch mean the same thing. In skateboarding, however, they mean different things. In skateboarding, riding fakie means rolling backward while in your normal stance. You'll be popping off of your strong foot, as you normally would.

Pushing

AH, PUSH IT. PUSH IT GOOD. PUSH IT REAL GOOD. (IS A SALT N PEPA REFERENCE TOO OLD? AM I DATING MYSELF?)

Now that you've figured out which way you ride, it's time to learn how to get that board moving. Pushing is a pretty simple process: you put one foot on the board, the other on the ground and push yourself along. However, like most things in skateboarding, you can look pretty stupid doing it the wrong way.

Yes, there is, arguably, a "wrong" way to push, which is referred to as "pushing mongo." It's when the back foot is over the back truck and the front foot pushes. It makes you look like some sort of caveman, and I don't recommend it.

Please just follow the steps at right. They'll save you from scorn and ridicule at the skate park. Don't attempt anything fancy when you push — keep it simple.

Stopping

SOMETIMES YOU NEED TO STOP ROLLING.
SOMETIMES YOU NEED TO STOP ROLLING IN A HURRY.

There's two ways to stop: the slow, easy I've-got-plenty-of-time-to-slow-down stop, and the quick, hard if-I-don't-reach-an-immediate-standstill-I'm-going-to-run-face-first-into-that-wall stop.

FOOT DRAG
The slow and easy way is the foot drag.

1 You're riding along, and you see someone in the distance you want to stop and talk to.

2 Put your weight on your front foot, keeping it on the board, and gently hover your pushing foot above the ground by your back wheels. Don't let your foot touch the wheels — it ends badly.

3 Slowly lower your back foot until you feel friction between it and the ground. Don't just stomp your foot down though, or you're going to have your legs ripped in half like a wishbone.

4 Steadily add pressure so you slow down gradually.

5 Once you've slowed down to a near stop, shift your weight to your pushing leg and stomp down so you come to a dead stop.

POWERSLIDE

The not-so-easy emergency stop is the powerslide. You can also use this method to slow down while bombing hills.

1 You're riding along, and you notice a brick wall's suddenly appeared in front of you. You need to stop.

3 With both feet facing outward, carve into a frontside turn so your board runs perpendicular to your original direction of travel.

4 Quickly dig in your heels so your board stays perpendicular.

5 Lean back and keep your heels dug in and the board perpendicular until you come to a screeching stop. You should adjust your weight once you've slowed down or you'll fall flat on your butt.

TAIL SKID

Another way to stop is the tail skid. Here, the heel is what's most important because it's what will stop you. The friction between the pavement and the rubber on your shoe, more so than the tail of the board, is what slows you down. Rubber is, after all, stickier than UV-coated wood.

1 Move your back foot to the back of the board. Put the ball of that foot on the tail and hang your heel off the edge.

3 Force your back foot to the ground with all your weight on it so the board and your heel are scraping the ground.

6 Lean back into it a little (not forward, obviously) to adjust for the change in speed until you reach a dead stop.

Kicking the Board Up

YOU'RE DONE SKATING AND YOU WANT TO GO HOME. GO HOME WITH A BIT OF STYLE.

You've had a long day of looking like a donkey with an inner ear disorder (it's okay kid, you're allowed to suck for the first couple months), and you just want to crash on the couch and veg out for a while. Maybe eat some cereal or something.

Instead of hopping off your board and leaning *all* the way to the ground to pick it up like a chump, might I suggest kicking that bad boy up to save yourself some work? There are two ways to work kids: there's working hard (reaching over and picking your board up) and working smart (kicking it up into your hand).

I suggest the path of least resistance and most style.

2 First, put your foot on the tail.

3 Then, push down sharply, slapping the tail down quickly against the ground. That will pop the nose up toward you.

4 Move your foot out of the way after you slap it down so your toes don't stop the board from coming all the way up.

5 Have your hand out and ready to catch your board, or you'll get the nose straight to the tender parts.

Go inside, kick back and crack a soda. You earned it.

Falling

YES, THERE ARE GOOD WAYS AND BAD WAYS TO HIT THE GROUND.

You've seen it on YouTube, and you've seen it on *America's Funniest Home Videos*, some poor kid bails midway through a trick and gets a crotch full of rail or a face full of cement.

Sadly kids, you're going to have to accept that you're going to fall off your skateboard. You are also going to get hurt. It's part of the learning process. Every pro skateboarder spends the vast majority of the day falling too, if that makes you feel any better.

ROCKS AND CRACKS

These hazards are the skateboarder's worst enemy. Riding over a rock or a crack unawares will send just about any skateboarder head first into something, so be aware of what you're rolling on. Avoid rocks at all costs. Try to avoid cracks but if you can't, lift your front wheels up and "hop," allowing your back wheels to run over the crack with less weight than normal. It's usually a perfect solution.

ACCEPT THAT YOU ARE NO LONGER ON YOUR BOARD

Once you've fallen there's nothing you can do about it. Don't try to fight it. Putting your arms out to catch yourself is a common mistake, which usually results in a dislocated shoulder or elbow, or a broken bone.

COMBAT ROLL

I admit, I don't actually think this is the following maneuver's name, but it's my pet name for it. Have you've ever seen stuntmen in movies jump out of moving cars? Well, this move is similar, except your board has stopped and you're the only thing moving, flying forward. Here's how to deal with it:

1 As you fly in midair (no doubt swearing at your board), tuck your chin into your chest and your arms into your body. As one friend of mine told me, "I've found it's better to take your leading arm and to palm the back of your skull with your hand, which protects your dome piece." I'd heed his advice.

2 Roll into the ground with your shoulder, letting it take the impact. Trust me, it's better than letting your wrist or elbow take the fall.

3 Go limp and try to roll with the inertia you've gathered. It'll still be painful, but it'll hurt a lot less.

Tic Tac

IT HAS NOTHING TO DO WITH THE MINTS AND EVERYTHING TO DO WITH FREESTYLE.

Way back in skateboarding's days of headbands and short shorts, people used to have to tic tac a lot because skaters would get points deducted if their feet hit the floor during freestyle competitions (the ones with pylons you see in old 60s skate photos). You couldn't push yourself along. Seems silly now, I know, but that was the way it was back then.

Surviving that not-always-awesome period of skateboarding is the tic tac, which is a pretty useful little trick (though it ain't much of a trick).

If you're standing still on your board, you can tic tac to pick up speed or maintain momentum. They're pretty easy to pick up because they're basically kick turns, just repeated over and over again. So let's get to it.

3 Lift your front wheels slightly by gently leaning back on the tail. Keep your front foot touching the board. This is the "tic."

5 Once the wheels are up, pull your board to either the left or right with your front foot using the grip tape. Then put the wheels back down. This is the "tac."

7 Quickly repeat step three — tic.

9 Quickly repeat step five in the opposite direction — tac.

Repeat the steps until you have a quasi-slithering motion going and have gathered momentum.

Turning

'CAUSE ROLLING IN A STRAIGHT LINE ALL DAY IS PRETTY BORING.

Now that you've learned how to stand on your board and push yourself along, the next thing on the list of basics is turning.

Turning is, obviously, key to maneuvering and lining yourself up for tricks. And it looks cool too. (It's science — we don't make this stuff up. They've done studies to prove it.)

One thing to note is how you've got your trucks tuned. It's much easier to turn with loose trucks than it is with tight trucks. So if you're having a hard time turning, loosen your trucks up a bit.

Like a great many things in life, there's more than one way to turn, and some ways are better than others.

CARVING

This is the easiest way to change your direction. There's two ways to place your feet, but the turn is essentially the same.

1 Roll along with one foot forward or both pointing to the side. Keep your knees bent.

2 Shift your weight to your heel or toes in the direction you want to turn, leaning your body slightly.

3 The shift in weight on the trucks and wheels will send you in your desired direction.

KICK TURN

Not the prettiest way to turn, but sometimes you just have to do them, especially when you don't have enough room or momentum to carve.

1 As you roll, place your back foot between the bolts and tail. Lean in the direction you want to go and lift your front foot up slightly, keeping your normal amount of weight on your back foot. This movement will send the nose of the board upward.

2 Now that the front of the board is in the air it's easier to move, so kick or pull it in the direction you want to go, using the grip tape to hold the board.

3 Put enough weight on your front foot to bring the board down. Repeat as needed.

Ollie

THE MOST FUNDAMENTAL ELEMENT OF MODERN SKATEBOARDING IS ALSO THE HARDEST TO LEARN.

4

It's a simple little illusion: make the board look like it's sticking to your feet as you jump in the air. Simple, but for over 30 years the ollie has been the basis of modern street skating.

Ever since Allan "Ollie" Gelfand first "popped" his board off the ground in the Underbowl at Skateboard USA back in 1977, skateboarders have followed suit and taken it to the streets. That simple act opened up the world to skateboarders. No longer were we confined to rolling around, freestyling or carving in pools. Suddenly we were airborne, and everything about skateboarding changed.

The revolution that is "street" skateboarding began with the ollie. Hopping up onto benches, ledges and handrails to do grinds and slides and popping up to do flip tricks — things that are so essential to the skateboarding you see today — wouldn't be possible without that one little trick, the ollie. It's the most important trick to learn.

You'll be doing thousands of ollies over the years as a skateboarder, so you'd better get good at them. And that's not to say ollies are easy

because, believe me, they're not. The ollie, while your starting point for pretty much everything, takes a lot of practice to perfect. It's a lot like riding a bike — once you figure it out, you'll never forget how to do it (but you might stink at it for a while).

Everything you want to do with your board happens at least a foot in the air. The bigger you pop, the more time you've got to land whatever flip trick you want to try and the bigger the ledge or rail you can jump onto. It may all sound like gibberish now, but you'll be stoked later on.

So, without further ado, the ollie.

9

how-to:

1 Crouch down on your board with the ball of your back foot on the tail, the heel of your back foot hanging off to the side and your front foot in the middle of your board.

2 In one quick motion, jump up off your back foot to send the nose of the board up toward you. Do not let that back foot (and the tail) touch the ground for long. Treat it as if you're touching something to see if it's hot — you have to make contact with the ground, but not long enough to get burned.

3 When the nose jumps up toward you, drag your front foot along the grip tape toward the nose to lift the board with you. Remember to suck your back leg up too, so it's always above the board.

4 By now your board should be on it's way up in the air, and your feet should be hovering on or near the bolts of the trucks.

5 Guide the board with your feet so it's parallel to the rest of your body, keeping it as level as you can. Don't let the board get away from you — keep those feet where they're supposed to be, the bolts.

7 Keep your feet centered and remember to bend your knees to absorb the impact of your landing (otherwise you'll feel really, really old when you're 30). Once you're on the ground, roll away and look for someone to high five.

OLLIE

Nollie

MEET THE OLLIE'S EVIL BACKWARD TWIN.

The best way to describe a nollie, is that it's the mirror image of an ollie. It's ass backward (or forward, if you want to get all literal on me).

In a nutshell, instead of slapping your tail down, you'll be doing it to your nose. Thus why it's called a nollie. It's a nose ollie.

That said, if you remember how hard it was to land ollies consistently, meet your newest frustration. Nollies are very hard to master, as everything is going on behind you.

It goes against your nature to, while rolling forward, look at your back foot and try to concentrate on it. Not to mention, it's a lot easier for the board to get away from you, when it's behind you.

So the secret to nollies is getting the board in front of you as much as possible. When you kick the board down (just like you did with the ollie), you also kick it out in front of you. This way, it's easier to see what's going on, and to keep control of your board.

4

3

2

1

how-to:

1 Crouch down on your board, with your front foot on the nose and your back foot just before the back bolts of the board.

2 This part is basically the same as the ollie, but backward. Kick down on your board with your front foot. That's going to send the tail of the board up toward you. Don't let the front foot touch the ground for long — it's the same quick motion as the ollie. At the same time as you kick

it down, kick it out in front of you as much as you can.

3 As the tail jumps up toward you, drag your back foot from the middle of the board, along the grip tape, back toward the tail, lifting it up with you. Remember to tuck your front foot up.

4 By now your board should be on it's way up in the air, with your feet hovering on or near the bolts of your trucks.

6 Guide the board parallel with your feet to the rest of your body, and keep it as level as you can. Don't let the board get away from you — keep those feet on the bolts.

8 Keep your feet centered and remember to bend those knees to absorb the impact of your landing.

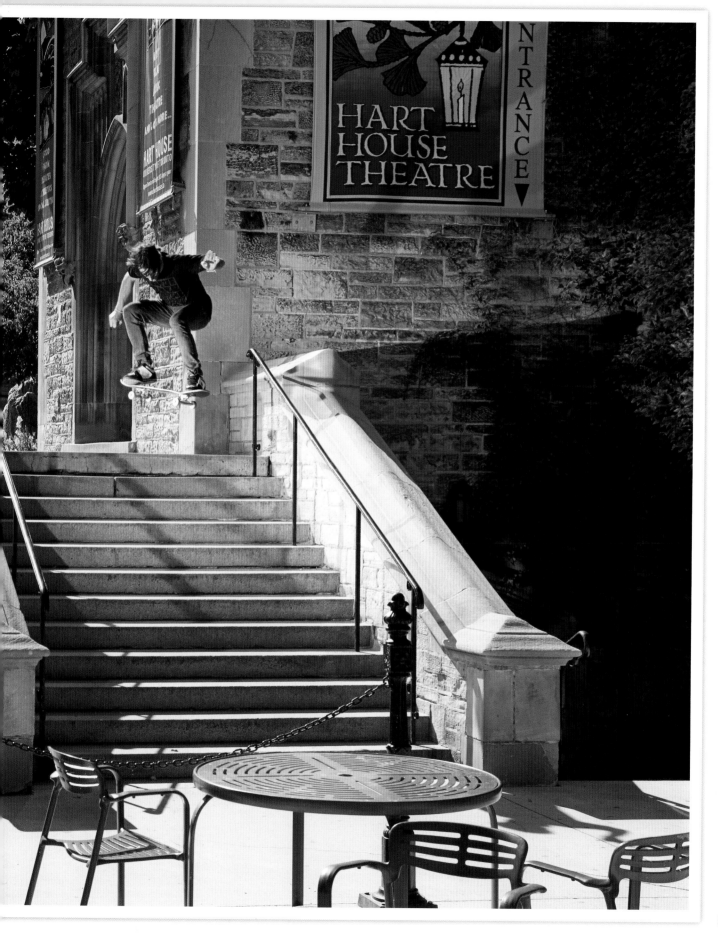

Manual

IT'S LIKE RIDING A BIKE (IF YOUR BIKE CONSTANTLY TRIES TO THROW YOU OFF).

A manual is a balancing act: balancing yourself on one set of wheels instead of two, essentially turning your board into a teeter-totter on wheels. Sounds easy, right? Well, you may only be able to hang on to one for a few feet, if that. And if you lose your balance, odds are the board will dart out from under you, sending you either face or butt first into the concrete. Manuals are fun, but they're quick to hurt.

There are two types of manuals (or mannies, as they're often called) — the nose manual and the regular manual. I'm going to assume that, having read the ollie and nollie sections, once you've figured out how to do a regular manny you'll be able to figure out how to do a nose manny: it's a manual, just on the nose of your board.

If you want to practice on flat first (which is a good idea) instead of a manny pad, as pictured, ignore step three.

On to the manual.

how-to:

1 Get some decent speed. You don't want to be going too fast while you're learning mannies, but you can't be dawdling either. Moderate speed is your friend.

3 Ollie onto the box, but instead of putting your front wheels down, keep them up and land on your back wheels.

5 Keep your back foot on the tail and your front foot just behind the front bolts. The idea is to balance on your back truck with both feet pointing to the side.

6 Keep a little extra weight on your back foot to hold the nose up a little, but not enough weight to force the tail to the ground. You want to have your back leg fairly straight and your front leg bent as needed to counter-balance. The secret is finding the sweet spot on your back truck that will keep you level.

7 Use your arms to help counter-balance yourself. If you start to dip forward while manualing, drop your back arm to pull the nose back up (and vice versa for nose manuals).

8 Once you've found the sweet spot, hold on for as long as you can. If you feel yourself losing it, shift your weight forward rather than backward, as you'll be less likely to bail.

10 When you're done showing off, shift your weight to your front foot and put your front wheels down. If you're on a curb or manny pad, drop off the edge and put your front wheels down as you hop off.

Transition Basics

KICKERS AND RAMPS AND POOLS, OH MY!

Ask any skater and they'll tell you how much fun it is to skate transition. Even dedicated street skaters get excited when someone talks about going to a mini-ramp for a session. It's a nice change from pushing around at a skate park or a spot. Ramps give skaters a bit of a break from what they're used to and the chance to try new sets of tricks in a totally different setting.

But transition isn't just mini-ramps. Everything I talk about in the following section can be applied to any sort of transition skating — from those giant 60-foot (1.83 m) vert ramps to small quarter pipes to mini-ramps and pools.

That said, any way you skate it, transition can be a little sketchy sometimes. Even Danny Way, the guy who's dropped into a vert ramp from a helicopter and jumped the Great Wall of China on a skateboard, can have a four-foot (1.2 m) mini-ramp kick his ass if he isn't careful.

While it's fun as all hell, it's also easy to face plant skating transition. You're generally skating fast, and if you miss even the most simple of moves, you're going to bail hard. There isn't much you can do — it's the price you pay for having fun. So pay attention to the basics, practice with a helmet until you get the hang of it and concentrate on not falling.

TERMS YOU NEED TO KNOW

DECK The top part of a ramp or a pool, where you stand before dropping in. Not to be confused with a skate deck, which is another term for the board of a skateboard.

COPING The lip at the top of the transition. On a ramp, it's the metal tube that joins the deck and the ramp. It's where grinds and slides are performed.

FLAT BOTTOM (OR FLAT) Like a lot of things in skateboarding, this term is pretty self-explanatory. The flat bottom is the flat part of the ramp, between the two transitions.

TRANSITION (OR TRANNY) This is what makes a ramp a ramp. The transition is the curved part of the ramp, between the coping and flat bottom. It's the part you'll be riding up and down on.

Dropping In

THE SCARIEST THING YOU'LL LEARN ON A BOARD.

If, like me, you're addicted to online videos of people face planting, you've no doubt seen people failing miserably at dropping in. Be it the dad who thought he'd "show these young whippersnappers how easy that skateboarding thing is" or the guy whose skills didn't match his ego, it inevitably ends with someone's face bouncing off of Masonite because he didn't know how to drop in properly.

Dropping in is, in a word, intimidating. You can bail out on every other trick, but when dropping into transition there's no second chance. Halfway through a kick flip you can decide to throw your feet to either side, and you'll land on the ground with no injury. When dropping in, once you put that front foot on your board, you're going down, one way or the other. It's by far the scariest thing you'll learn from this book.

But that leads me to the most important part of dropping in — commitment. Once you're leaning forward, you must eliminate the fear of falling from your mind. If you hesitate and lean backward, you're going to fall 10 times out of 10.

The steps to drop in follow, so all you need now is a lot of guts and a helmet until you get it right.

how-to:

1 Put your board down with the tail and back truck resting on the coping and hold it in place with your pushing foot.

3 That was the easy part, and here's where the trick gets tricky. When you're ready to take the plunge, put your front foot with your toes to the side on top of the front bolts of your board.

5 As you place your front foot, in one swift motion shift your weight from your back foot to your front foot, bringing your whole body forward. Don't throw too much weight either way or you'll bail. Like everything in skateboarding, there's a sweet spot in the shifting of balance. And you can't hesitate — commit yourself to riding it out.

9 If you haven't fallen, congrats, you've just dropped in.

Pumping

IT SHOULD REALLY BE CALLED SQUATTING…

Dropping into a ramp or pool will give you enough momentum to roll back and forth between the copings once or twice. After that you'll be losing speed and unable to reach the coping or get back on top of the deck.

You have to learn how to get some of the speed you've lost back, and the best way is to pump. Don't ever try to push on transition — it's stupidly dangerous.

Pumping is hard to describe, but I'll do my best; it's a lot like pumping on a swing set. You're shifting your body weight to gain momentum. There's a sweet spot at the start and end of the transition, which is where you'll get all your speed from if you learn to use it right.

how-to:

1 As you roll up the transition, straighten your legs out slightly from their normal, crouched, position.

6 When you get as high as you can up the tranny and feel yourself about to come back down, squat.

9 Once you reach the sweet spot of the transition (as pictured), straighten your legs out quickly. This quick motion, from squatting to standing while rolling through the sweet spot, will propel you forward.

10 When you reach the other side, repeat steps one through three until you can reach above the coping.

Kick Turn on Transition

THE BEST TURN IS ALSO YOUR ONLY TURN.

Kick turns are pretty much your only turning option on most transitions. Carving can only be done in a pool where you've got room to maneuver. You've got a limited amount of turning space on mini-ramps and quarter pipes, thus why kick turns are so important.

Kick turns also come in handy when you don't have enough speed to reach the coping and want to avoid rolling back into the transition fakie. They're an easy move that'll keep you facing the right way when skating ramps.

Here's how they go.

how-to:

1 While you roll, place your back foot between the bolts and tail.

2 As you ride up the transition, prepare to turn when you feel yourself starting to lose momentum.

3 Lean in the direction you want to go, lift your front foot up slightly and keep your normal amount of weight on your back foot, which will send the nose of the board upward.

5 The front of the board will be easier to move when it is up in the air, so kick or pull it in the direction you want to go by putting your foot back on it and using the grip tape to hold your foot to the board.

6 Pivot on the back truck until you've turned around completely or turned enough to power through until you're straightened back out.

9 Continue riding down the ramp like a champ.

Nose and Tail Stalls

THE TRANSITIONS ON TRANSITION.

After you've dropped in on a mini-ramp (or any other tranny), you've got about two seconds to figure out your next move before you hit the other coping. That's why we've got stalls — they give us all a little respite during day-to-day sessions.

The fundamental stalls are nose and tail stalls. With both of these stalls you'll be going back to the same position you were in before you dropped in: resting with the nose or tail on top of the coping and your wheels flush against it.

Pictured here is the tail stall, but a nose stall is the same trick in reverse, so I've made the instructions work for both.

how-to:

1 Ride up to the coping with your forward foot on the tail (for a tail stall) or the nose (for a nose stall).

2 Once your wheels are about to hit the coping, push your forward foot down onto the coping so the tail or nose hits the top of it.

3 Shift your weight onto your forward foot so that you rest on the coping for a second or two.

7 When you want to drop back in, shift your weight away from the coping (just like dropping in) and let gravity do the rest.

Axle Stall

SO, UM, YEAH, YOU LIKE SKATEBOARDING? YEAH, TOTALLY, ME TOO… SO, WHAT ELSE IS NEW?

J Just as the name suggests, when you do an axle stall you come to a stop on the coping, resting on both trucks. It looks like a 50-50 grind (see page 94), except that, of course, you're not moving.

The most important thing about stalls is how you ride into them, because the only thing keeping an axle stall from being a 50-50 grind is momentum. If you ride toward the coping with a lot of speed, you're going to end up grinding because your forward momentum will keep you moving.

However, if you ride straight up, or nearly straight up, all your momentum pushes you upward, and you can control it, making it easier to stop. Make sure you're riding in as straight a line as possible and not carving too harshly.

how-to:

1. Ride up to the coping, lifting the front truck slightly to ensure it clears the coping.

3. Let the back truck rest on top of the coping but do not clear it.

4. Next, turn your body and your board so you're lined up with the coping. Focus on balancing on the heel side of the back truck.

5. Once steady, lock yourself in by shifting your weight slightly and putting the front truck down on the coping. You might slide slightly, but, if you've come into the trick correctly, you should be pretty stationary at this point.

6. Balance on the coping for as long as you like, and remember to use your arms for balance. (If you've brought a sandwich or thermos with you, enjoy a snack or beverage.)

7. When you want to drop back in, balance on the back truck and lift the front truck off the coping. Pivot off the back truck, guiding the nose back down into the transition.

9. Shift your weight to your back foot and turn yourself back into the ramp. Ride on in.

Rock 'n Rolls

THROW YOUR HORNS IN THE AIR AND TEETER YOUR BOARD ON THE COPING.

It's not as flashy a trick as the name would suggest, but rock 'n rolls are fun to do. They're the trick you do in between harder tricks — a way to link your run together and give you time to think about what you want to do next.

So without further ado, ladies and gentlemen, please welcome to the stage: rock 'n rolls.

how-to:

3 As you roll up to the coping, keep your knees bent and go up high enough so that at least the middle of your board is over the coping.

5 Then, using the coping as a balancing point, "rock" your board and push the front wheels down on top of the deck with your front foot.

6 Once you hear the "ca-chunk" sound of the wheels hitting the deck, put weight on your back foot to lift the front wheels back off the deck and over the coping.

8 With the front wheels up, pivot off the back truck and turn yourself 180 degrees. The front wheels will be off the coping and you'll be facing the ramp nose first.

10 Once you've pivoted, put your front wheels back down and ride away.

nose of board

6

7

Tricks on Transition

IT'S NOT ALL JUST BACK AND FORTH...

Once you've mastered the art of skating coping to coping, and you're able to stall and carve your way around transition without killing yourself, it's time to throw a trick or two into your runs.

You'll want to start out slowly, with just one trick in your run. Don't try to throw down multiple tricks. You'll find out pretty quickly just how nerve-racking it is to get out of your "kick turn, stall, kick turn, pivot" routine.

Begin with some basic grinds and other tricks from this book. You'll know how to stall, so you'll know how to get up on the coping. Just apply the same principles to new tricks. Try a 50-50 in the middle of your run for starters. They're easy, relatively safe and you can bail out of them more often than not.

Then try something a little harder, such as a 5-0 grind, and then work your way up to something harder. Push yourself to try something new once you get a trick down. Not something insanely more difficult that will end with a broken bone, but something a little harder than what you've been doing.

The secret to learning new tricks isn't terribly sexy — it's practice. A lot of it.

Bro, where's the grabs?

There's something left out of this section, and that's grab tricks. Much like the name suggests, grab tricks involve grabbing your board while skating transition. There's a ton of grab and other transition tricks, which deserve a book of their own, but for now I'm assuming no kid just stepping on a board will be doing grabs.

Falling on Tranny

You will, inevitably, eat it on transition. Much like skating flat, you have to learn how to roll with it.

Here's a few tips to keep you from a trip to the ER (I also recommend the steps found in the Falling section of the Flat Ground chapter, see page 41).

Don't try to stop your fall Dude, you're done. You fell. Just accept it and don't fight it. Putting your arms out to catch yourself will only result in dislocating a shoulder or elbow, or possibly even breaking something.

Roll with it The best way to fall is to just go limp and try to roll with the inertia you've gathered. It will hurt a lot less.

It burns! It burns! Masonite, that slippery surface that covers skate ramps, burns when you fall on it. Concrete, the stuff that pools are made of, tears when you fall on it. Aside from wearing long sleeves and protective equipment, there's not much you can do to avoid street rash and Masonite burns.

Flip Tricks

Now that I've got you through the basics of skateboarding, here's where the actual fun happens: tricks. More specifically, flip tricks.

A flip trick is, and it pains me to say it, a trick where the board flips (you'd think it was pretty obvious, but let's just say some people don't get it). The board can flip top over bottom, nose to tail or vice versa. Pretty simple.

But the flip trick's place in the pantheon of skateboarding couldn't be bigger — they started the revolution of street skating and, even today, continue to grow and evolve. There are probably only a handful of skaters in the world who can say they can do every flip trick, and they're probably lying.

Here you'll learn some flip-trick fundamentals. Things that, once learned, you can keep changing up and varying to make new tricks (new to you, at least).

All of these tricks can be done in a ton of different ways. I don't want to say you're never going to get bored of them, but getting them all on lock is going to take you a sweet long time (at least until I convince the publisher to let me do a sequel).

Without further ado, let's get that board flipping.

Kick Flip

BETTER FLIPPING THROUGH KICKING.

A kick flip can be stylish as all hell if done right. Done wrong, however, it will look like you have no muscular coordination whatsoever.

A kick flip is done by spinning the board top over bottom for a full 360 degrees. The nose and tail stay in the same direction they were when you rode into the trick — your board is flipping from left to right, toward your toes.

Height is what's most important. The higher you can pop your ollie, the more time you have to flip and catch your board. Make sure you have your ollies on lock before you try to kick flip. Trust me, it'll help.

how-to:

1 First off, get a comfortable amount of speed.

2 Ollie up, making sure you pop as far off the ground as possible. The higher you are, the more time your board has to rotate (and the more time you have to catch it).

3 This next step is the most important part of the trick. As you drag your front foot forward in the ollie to bring the board up, kick toward the heel side of the nose to make it flip. This kick is going to send the board underneath you, giving you the most height possible.

4 Keep your feet up and your eyes on your board as it rotates below you. You'll see the bottom of your board as it turns.

6 Once it rotates a full flip (360 degrees) and you start to see grip tape beneath you again, get your feet in position to catch the board. As always, aim to have your feet on, or at least near, the bolts.

7 When you've caught the board with your back foot, get your front foot on it, both feet squarely on the bolts. Keep your knees bent and prepare for landing.

8 Try to even the board out so you land on all four wheels at the same time (or as close as possible to the same time).

9 Stomp down and roll away happy.

KICK FLIP

Heel Flip

THE SAME OLD FLIP, ONLY DIFFERENT.

9

8

7

6

As with a lot of skateboard tricks, variation makes old flips fresh. Take the heel flip, which is pretty much the same idea as the kick flip, but with a slight change in maneuver.

What's consistent? You're going to ollie and rotate your board by kicking it out to the side as you lift it up.

What's the change that makes it new? Instead of kicking the board toward you with your toe, you're going to kick it away from you with your heel.

Thus, the name "heel flip." Here's how you do it.

how-to:

1 First off, get a decent amount of speed and position your feet for an ollie, but instead of centering your front foot on the board, hang your toes off slightly, with the ball of your foot on the heel edge of the tail.

3 Ollie up off the ground. Height is also important for heel flips, so make sure you get as far off the ground as possible. The higher you are, the more time you've got to catch your board.

4 Here's the most important part of the trick: as you drag your toe forward in the ollie to bring the board up, kick it out in front of you using the ball and heel of your foot. This kick is going to make the board flip underneath you.

5 Keep your feet up and your eyes on your board as it rotates below you. You'll see the bottom of your board as it turns. (If, like Morgan, you can look as though you're jump kicking someone, do so.)

6 Once your board rotates a full spin and you start to see grip tape beneath you again, catch it with your back foot. As always, aim to have your feet on, or near, the bolts.

8 With your feet squarely on the bolts, keep your knees bent and prepare for landing.

9 Stomp down and roll away.

Pop Shove-It

MUCH LIKE PREVIOUS TRICKS, ITS NAME INDICATES WHAT YOU'LL BE DOING.

Unlike kick flips and heel flips, you don't rotate your board top to bottom when doing a pop shove-it. You rotate it nose to tail for 180 degrees, keeping the wheels facing the ground and the grip tape facing up.

It takes a little more coordination than kick or heel flips, as you use both feet to make your board rotate and change how you pop the board up. It sounds complicated but don't sweat it. Pop shoves aren't really intense once you get the hang of them — besides, you should save your sweating for 360 and varial flips.

Here's how to do a pop shove-it.

how-to:

1 First off, get a comfortable amount of speed.

2 This next step is the "pop," the most important part of the trick. Keep your back foot closer to the toe-side edge of the board than you would for an ollie, with your big toe almost hanging over the side. Instead of popping the board up by stomping your back foot down, as you would for an ollie, use the toes of your back foot to slap the board down and "scoop" it out behind you in one quick motion.

3 Once you've "scooped" the board, you won't be bringing the nose up with your front foot, as you would for an ollie. The scoop will not only send the nose up but also turn it slightly, so all you need to do is lightly kick the nose in the direction it is turning with your front foot. This kick is going to help rotate the tail of the board behind you. It's the "shove-it" part of the trick.

5 Keep your feet up and your eyes on your board as it rotates below you.

6 Once the board's tail is underneath your front foot and the nose is under your back foot, catch the board with your front foot and bring it back beneath your back foot. As always, aim to have your feet on, or near, the bolts.

7 With your feet squarely on the bolts, keep your knees bent and prepare for landing. Keep in mind that you'll be landing fakie.

9 Stomp down and roll away fakie.

POP SHOVE-IT

Varial Flip

COMBINING TWO THINGS TO MAKE ONE THING WITH SLIGHTLY MORE FLAIR.

Here we're going to combine what you learned with the kick flip and pop shove-it and mash them together to make a new trick, the varial flip. You're going to be both rotating the board from nose to tail and flipping it from top to bottom in one quick little trick.

It's a little more complicated than either the kick flip or pop shove, but that's what skateboarding is all about — taking two individual tricks, putting them together and acting as though you invented a whole new trick. If you don't like it, take up chess, or knitting.

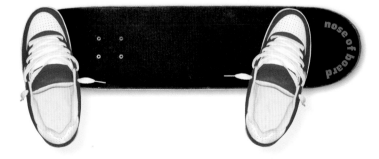

how-to:

1 First off, get a comfortable amount of speed.

3 As you stomp your back foot down to pop the board up, scoop it out behind you with your back toes, as you would for a pop shove. This move is going to rotate the tail of the board behind you.

4 Then, just as for an ollie, drag your front foot up the board, but then kick it out as you do in a kick flip. This kick is what makes the varial different from the pop-shove — you're adding a kick flip to the pop shove.

5 Keep your feet up and your eyes on your board as it rotates below you.

6 Once the board's tail is underneath your front foot and the nose is under your back foot, get your feet in position to catch the board. As always, aim to have your feet on, or near, the bolts.

7 With your feet squarely on the bolts, keep your knees bent and prepare for landing.

9 Stomp down and roll away happy.

360 Flip

OR, AS IT'S ALSO KNOWN, THE TRE FLIP, THREE FLIP AND 360 KICK FLIP.

I hate to break it to you, but the easy tricks are over. This last flip trick is pretty challenging, even for seasoned skaters. We're going to combine what you learned for the varial flip, kick flip and pop shove-it and mash them together into one trick: the 360 flip.

The only difference is, unlike the varial flip or pop shove-it, you'll be rotating the board a full 360 degrees underneath you, instead of just 180 degrees. It means you'll be landing on the board the same way you were before takeoff.

You may now freak out. When you're done crying, keep reading to learn how to do them right.

5

4

10

9

how-to:

1. First off, get a decent amount of speed.

3. Pop the board up behind you with your back foot as you do for the pop shove — instead of just slapping the board, "scoop" it up — but scrape the tail in a quick half-circle motion with enough juice to bring it around 360 degrees.

4. Next is the crux of the trick, done quickly after step three. Once you scoop the tail (which will bring the nose up a little), kick it out with your front foot, as you do for the varial flip. This will flip the board top over bottom while it spins from tail to nose.

5. Keep your feet up and your eyes on your board to keep track of all the spinning and rotation happening below you.

7. Once the board rotates enough for the nose to be underneath your front foot with the grip side up, catch it with your front foot and bring it back underneath your back foot. As always, aim to have your feet on, or near, the bolts.

8. With your feet squarely over the bolts, keep your knees bent and prepare for landing.

10. Stomp down, roll away and look for someone to high five.

CUSTOMER PARKING

Grinds

In the annals of skateboarding history, there have been some pretty iconic images, and a lot of them have been grinds. But that wasn't always the case. Until they were made popular during the late 80s, you'd rarely see someone grinding something.

Nowadays, seeing someone huck themselves down a flight of stairs to grind a handrail is fairly common, yet still pretty mind blowing. There's nothing quite like the sound of metal grinding on metal. It's no wonder most kids equate that with skateboarding.

Grinding is balancing on a truck (or both trucks, depending on the trick) and sliding along an object. You can grind pretty much anything: metal handrails, concrete or marble ledges, even wooden benches. Depending on the obstacle, you can lube it up with curb wax or a candle so the grind is smoother and easier.

There are a few things you should keep in mind when attempting any grind. Firstly, make sure the obstacle is low enough so that you can ollie high enough above it to have time to move your feet and board. You're not going to get very far with your grinds until your ollies are on point.

Also, keep in mind that anything you can slide on, you can grind on. If you've got a ledge or rail that you're comfortable sliding, start your grinds on it. As always, start with something small and work your way up.

Most of the landings pictured in this chapter are at a downward slope. You're not normally going to find slopes while skating street, so remember that you'll have to bring the nose of your board up on regular, even, landings.

Now let's wreck the trucks your mom just paid $50 for, shall we?

FRONTSIDE AND BACKSIDE: A CONFUSING LOVE STORY

All the tricks covered in this section (with the exception of smith grinds) are described backside for the sake of simplicity. No doubt you're asking yourself what I'm talking about. Frontside and backside describe how you ride up to an obstacle — the difference is the way you're facing before you grind or slide something. Backside you'll be leading up to the obstacle with your heels to it. Frontside you'll be running up with your toes toward it. Outside of that, the tricks are done the same way. Frontside tricks are generally a little harder to do, so we'll focus on the easy ones for now. It might be a little confusing at first (which is why I'm concentrating on backside tricks), but trust me, it'll all make sense soon enough.

50-50 Grind

YOU'VE GOT GOOD ODDS ON THIS ONE, EVEN IF YOUR LUCK IS AWFUL.

This one is by far the easiest grind you're going to learn. Remember the axle stall from the Transition chapter? This is the same thing, except you move fast instead of standing still.

The secret to the 50-50 grind is a combination of speed and balance. You've got to be rolling along at a decent speed to avoid stalling on the obstacle, and you've got to keep your weight evenly spread out on both feet and centered on the obstacle to avoid falling.

Your shoulders should always be parallel with whatever you are grinding. Another thing you should keep in mind with all of these tricks is to make sure you're picking an obstacle that's low enough for you to ollie on top of. No sense trying to grind something you can't reach — you're just going to hurt yourself. So if you can't reach anything, go back and get your ollies higher.

Now, on to 50-50s.

how-to:

1 Line yourself up with your obstacle after getting some decent speed.

3 Ollie up and over what you intend to grind.

5 Once you're up, push your board down with both feet and lock the trucks onto whatever you're grinding. Try to get both trucks on at the same time if you can.

6 Use your arms to balance yourself as you grind the hell out of that thing. Keep your shoulders parallel with the obstacle.

8 Grind straight off the end of the obstacle, lifting the front truck off the obstacle so you can land evenly.

9 As you head toward the ground, try to put all four wheels on the ground at the same time.

10 Roll away and look for someone to high five.

50-50 GRIND

5-0 Grind

LIKE THE 70s COP SHOW SET IN HAWAII, YOU PRONOUNCE IT "FIVE OH."

To step things up a bit, I'm going to run you through the wonderful world of 5-0 grinds. They're easy to explain, but that's not to say they're easy to do. They're similar to 50-50 grinds, only when doing 5-0s you're keeping the front truck from touching whatever obstacle you're skating.

Again, pick an obstacle that's low enough for you to ollie on top of — you'll just hurt yourself if you try to grind something you can't reach. If you want to cheat and put the tail down during the grind, it's okay, you won't bail, but it's bad style. If you want to impress, learn to keep that tail up and balance your board as you do during a manual.

how-to:

1 Line yourself up with your obstacle, and have some decent speed going.

3 Ollie up and over what you intend to grind.

4 Once you're up, push your back foot down and lock the back truck onto whatever you're grinding. Keep the nose of your board up and rest your front foot on it.

5 Use your arms to balance yourself. Keep your shoulders parallel with the obstacle and your knees slightly bent.

6 As you grind, keep your eyes on your landing. When you see the end coming, get ready.

8 Allow yourself to grind right off the obstacle. Push the front truck down to level out your board as you get free of the grind so you land evenly.

9 As you head toward the ground, try to put all four wheels down at the same time.

10 Roll away stoked.

3.0 GRIND

Nose Grind

NOT THE MOST ORIGINAL GRIND, BUT STILL PRETTY RAD.

I'm about to drop a bomb on you, so prepare yourself: a nose grind is a 5-0 grind done on the front truck. Sorry if this is shattering any illusions you had about the strange and ambiguous world of the nose grind, but that's all it is. We all have to find these things out sooner or later, just like the fact that the Tooth Fairy and the Easter Bunny are the same person — mom or dad. Wait, you did know it was your parents, right?

If you can land 5-0s consistently, you should be able to lock nose grinds. Here's how you do them.

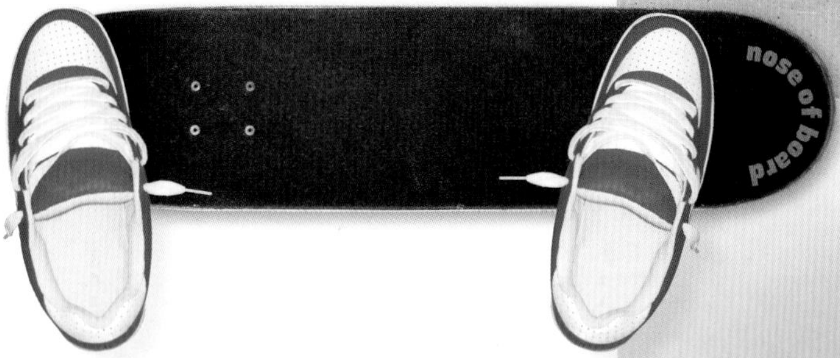

nose of board

5

4

10

9

1 Work yourself up to a good speed, and line yourself up with your obstacle.

3 Ollie up and over what you intend to grind.

4 Once you're up, push your front foot down and lock the front truck onto whatever you're grinding. Your front foot should be between the nose and front bolts, and your back foot should be over your back bolts.

5 Don't cheat by letting your nose drag — keep it up (as with a nose manual). The tail should be parallel to the obstacle during the entire grind.

6 Use your arms to balance yourself on your front truck as you grind. Keep your shoulders parallel to the obstacle.

7 Watch for the end of the grind, and get yourself ready for your landing.

8 Grind straight off the end of the obstacle, giving it a slight nollie as the nose comes to the end. Wait for the tail to clear the obstacle, then straighten your board out and bring the tail down so you land evenly.

10 Roll away happy.

NOSE GRIND

Smith Grind

LOCK AND, UH, GRIND.

While it may not be the easiest grind to learn, the smith grind will be one of your go-to grinds once you've got it down, mostly because once into it, you're locked into it.

During a smith grind you grind on the back truck, while the front truck hangs off the side you rode in from and the toe-side edge of your board slides along the edge of the obstacle.

Once you get into a smith grind there's not much that can toss you out of it. The heel-side wheel holds the back truck steady, and while the middle of your board is sliding, the toe-side wheel keeps it from going anywhere. It's idiot proof. (Not to say you're an idiot if you don't get it quickly, but the only way you can fall out of a smith grind once into it is by putting too much weight forward.)

Smith grinds are the only frontside grind you'll learn in this book. Backside smith grinds are a little too tech for you just yet.

how-to:

1 Line yourself up frontside with your obstacle with some good speed.

2 Ollie up and above what you intend to grind.

3 Once you're up, position the nose of your board to the side of the obstacle and line up your back truck so it'll land directly on it. Keep your feet over the bolts.

4 When you land on the obstacle, grind on your back truck and slide on the toe-side edge of your board. All of your weight should be on your back foot and your back knee should be bent. Your front leg should jut out straight, with your toes pointing out and down, locking your board onto the obstacle.

5 Balance yourself with your arms and hang on. Keep those shoulders parallel to the obstacle.

7 When you reach the end, put a little extra pressure on your back foot to lift the nose up and then grind off the obstacle.

8 Once your back truck clears the obstacle, straighten out your board as you head toward the ground.

9 Try to put all four wheels on the ground at the same time.

10 Roll away and maybe find a bite to eat (you've earned it).

SMITH GRIND

Feeble Grind

IT MAY BE NAMED AFTER YOUR UPPER BODY MUSCLES…

Feeble grinds are, quite possibly, the best looking grind around. Stylish as a mother-scratcher when done correctly, they do, however, look stupid when done wrong.

The feeble grind is similar to the smith grind, except in a feeble the front of your board hangs over the opposite side of the bar (from where you rode in from) and in a smith it stays on the same side. They're a nice looking grind and fun to do. What more do you want?

So how about I quit babbling and teach you how to do the trick already?

how-to:

1 While rolling at a decent speed, line yourself up with your obstacle.

3 Ollie up and over what you intend to grind.

4 Once you're up, line up the middle of your board with the obstacle.

5 Land on your back truck, and as soon as it touches lean back and extend your front foot, so the bottom of your board rests on the obstacle.

Both the back truck and the center of your board should be on the obstacle, with the front truck hanging off to the side without touching it — if it touches, it'll mess you up.

6 Keep your feet over the bolts with more weight on your back foot than on your front foot. Once you're locked, use your arms to balance yourself on your front truck. Keep your shoulders parallel to the obstacle.

7 Watch for the end of the grind and get ready for a weird dismount (if skateboarders were gymnasts).

8 As you head toward the ground, straighten the board out and put all four wheels on the ground at the same time, if you can.

10 Roll away as though it was no big deal.

FEEBLE GRIND

Crooked Grind

KROOKED GRIND? NO, IT'S A CROOKED GRIND.

Most people credit pro skateboarder Eric Koston with inventing this trick (which is, however, wrong), so much so that some people call it a k-grind. Ignore these people. It's a crooked grind.

Similar to a nose grind, the only difference between the two is the angle at which the tail hangs off the obstacle. During a nose grind the tail is parallel with the obstacle, but in a crooked grind it juts out to the side, making balancing a little harder.

Also, the nose will drag on the obstacle, but if you're doing sloppy nose grinds the nose is likely dragging anyway. So, once again, laziness pays off for skateboarders.

On to the trick.

6

9

10

how-to:

1. Get some speed and line yourself up with your obstacle.

3. Ollie up and over it.

4. Once you're up, line up the nose and front truck with the obstacle and keep the tail hanging off the side at an angle. Your front foot should be between the front bolts and the nose.

5. Push your front foot down and lock the front truck onto whatever you're grinding, dragging the nose on the obstacle. Most of your weight should be on your front foot, and your back foot should be tucked up above the back bolts. (This positioning is the difference between a nose and a crooked grind. For a crooked grind, you're dragging the nose the whole time and the tail is hanging off to the side.)

6. Keep the tail hanging off the obstacle at an angle. Use your arms to balance yourself on the front truck, and keep your shoulders as square as you can with the obstacle (it's hard, but try).

7. Grind straight off the end of the obstacle.

8. Once you clear the end, straighten your board out and bring the tail down so you land evenly.

9. Try to put all four wheels down at the same time

10. Roll away like it don't mean nothin'.

CROOKED GRIND

Slides

Sliding isn't rocket science — you use your board's smooth, UV-finished underside to slide on something. When you think about it, it makes a lot more sense than trying to slide metal trucks on something. The bottom of your board is a slippery, low-friction surface — it was made to slide on.

For any slide trick, you need to be able to ollie higher than the obstacle you want to slide on, have plenty of wax on said obstacle and ride with enough speed to make sure you don't stall.

You should also be prepared to fall a lot. It takes a while to get the hang of distributing your weight properly. It's a bit finicky, but like everything in skateboarding, with a little practice you'll get it.

Secondly, don't be stupid and try to slide something huge, such as a 20-stair handrail, to impress your friends. Unless stupidity and large hospital bills impress your friends, you're going to be disappointed. You should not be skating anything over 1 to 2 feet (30 to 60 cm) tall for the foreseeable future. Pick an obstacle you can handle (such as a flat bar or curb) and work your way up.

FRONTSIDE AND BACKSIDE YEP — IT'S THE SAME EXPLANATION AS THE GRIND CHAPTER.

Once again, a little explanation. Everything covered in this chapter is described backside, for simplicity sake.

If you missed it on page 93, frontside and backside are how you ride up to an obstacle — the difference between the two is the way you're facing before you get up and grind or slide something.

Backside you'll be leading up to the obstacle with your heels facing it. Frontside you'll be running up with your toes toward it. Other than that, the tricks are the same.

Boardslide

THIS SLIDE IS TECHNICALLY A BACKSIDE BOARDSLIDE, EVEN THOUGH YOU'RE FACING FORWARD WHEN YOU SLIDE. WEIRD, ISN'T IT?

When it comes to slides, there isn't one easier than the boardslide. You've got a lot of forgiveness when sliding (except for that metal pole between your legs), and you're usually able to bail out of it if need be.

What's pictured here is a backside boardslide. I know, it's weird that a trick you do face-forward is "backside," but it's all in how you approach the obstacle — if your back's to it as you ride up to it, it's a backside trick.

I didn't just make that up. No, really. Read on, learn how to do the trick and see for yourself.

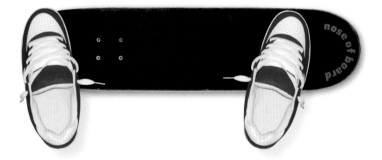

3

6

9

how-to:

1 Line yourself up with your heels facing the obstacle.

3 Ollie up and over it.

4 Once you're above the obstacle, put the front truck over to the other side (the opposite side from which you approached), so the center of your board is on the obstacle.

5 Keep your feet on the bolts and evenly distribute your weight on both feet. Bend your legs slightly and keep your shoulders facing the direction you're sliding — don't turn your back on the direction you're sliding.

6 Use your arms to balance yourself as you slide along like butter on a hot frying pan.

7 As you near the end of the obstacle, get ready to straighten yourself back out.

8 Once you pop off the end of the obstacle, twist yourself until you and your board are straightened out.

9 Try to land on both sets of wheels at the same time and roll away happy.

BOARDSLIDE

Lipslide

NO, CAPTAIN OBVIOUS, IT'S NOT A BOARDSLIDE.

9 8 7 6 5

nose of board

So you're thinking this slide looks a lot like a boardslide except he's facing backward as he slides . It does look a lot like a boardslide, but there is one big difference: rotation.

If you look at the first few frames, you'll notice that Morgan ollies up and over the rail then rotates 45 degrees before he starts sliding. There's your difference.

All it takes is an extra 45-degree rotation kids — that and a lot of pop in your ollie. At the risk of sounding like a broken record, I'll tell you again that you need to have a decent ollie to have any hope of landing any slide or grind.

Now pucker up and learn lipslides.

how-to:

1 Get some good speed and line yourself up to the obstacle with your heels facing it.

3 Ollie up and over what you intend to slide.

4 Once you're above it, twist your body and board until your back is facing the length of the obstacle. The tail should go over to the other side of the obstacle.

5 Once your board is over the obstacle, center it as evenly as you can. Keep your feet on the bolts and evenly distribute your weight on both feet. Bend both legs slightly.

6 Once you've landed and you're sliding, use your arms to balance yourself. Keep your head turned to the side so you can see both the end of the obstacle and your board. Slide to your little heart's content.

7 As you near the end of the obstacle, get ready to straighten yourself back out by putting your lead shoulder forward.

8 Once you pop off the end of the slide, twist yourself until you and your board are straightened out and nose first.

9 Try to land on both sets of wheels at the same time and roll away stoked.

LIPSLIDE

Tailslide

TRICKY? A BIT. FUN? YOU BET.

Now that you've got the hang of sliding on your board, with the aptly named boardslide, it's time to step it up a bit and try something a little more difficult: the tailslide.

The secret to learning tailslides is putting all of your weight on the tail. Your first instinct will be to put less weight on the tail to make you slide further, but that's a no-no.

How far you slide depends on how much speed you've got riding into it and how much wax is on the obstacle. Mind you, if it's a popular street spot or skate park, someone's likely taken care of the wax already, so you may not have to worry about it.

how-to:

1 Line yourself up with your heels facing the obstacle.

2 Ollie up and over it.

3 Once you're up, turn 90 degrees so the tail is over the obstacle, then kick the tail out to the side and onto the obstacle.

4 Keep one foot on the tail with most of your weight on it, but not enough weight to stall you. The tail should be flush against the obstacle, and your board should be perpendicular to the edge. Your other foot should be set lightly on the outside set of bolts.

5 Bend your legs and use your arms to balance yourself as you slide.

7 As you near the end of the obstacle, get ready to straighten yourself back out.

8 Once you pop off the end of the slide, turn your leading shoulder forward, which will help kick the nose out in front of you so you land straight.

9 Try to land on both sets of wheels at the same time and roll away.

TAIL SLIDE

Noseslide

IT'S EXACTLY WHAT IT SOUNDS LIKE. SLIDING ON YOUR NOSE. (YOUR BOARD'S NOSE, THAT IS.)

Next is the noseslide. Much like the boardslide, it's easy to do once you get the hang of it. Keep in mind that once you get up onto the obstacle all of your weight should be on the nose, and pretty much zero weight should be on the tail.

How far you slide doesn't depend on how you distribute your weight — it's how much speed you have and how much wax is on the obstacle. That said, start on something small and manageable, slather it with wax and get your speed up.

Now on to teaching you how to do something involving noses that doesn't include sticking a finger in them.

how-to:

1 Get a comfortable amount of speed and line yourself up with your heels facing the obstacle.

3 Ollie up and over it.

4 Once you're up, put the nose over to the other side of the obstacle. Your front foot should be on the nose and your back foot should be on the opposite set of bolts.

5 Bend both legs slightly. Keep the majority of your weight on your front foot, and once again find that sweet spot of weight distribution.

6 Use your arms to balance yourself as you slide.

7 As you near the end of the obstacle, get ready to straighten yourself back out.

8 Once you pop off the end, twist yourself until you and your board are straightened out and nose first.

10 Try to land on both sets of wheels at the same time and roll away happy.

Glossary

Am
Short for amateur, ams are the level below pro skateboarders. They make a living from skateboarding but don't have signature products (and so don't collect royalties).

Axle
The metal rod on a truck, which runs the width of the skate deck and from which the wheels hang.

Back Foot
Also known as the pushing foot, the back foot is normally placed behind the skater.

Backside
A trick in which the rider leads up to the obstacle with the heels facing it.

Bank to Bank
A skate obstacle with an inclined plane to a flat top to a declined plane.

Barrier
There are a couple of different types of plastic and concrete barriers, and depending on the setup skaters can grind, stall and slide on them.

Baseplate
The top of a truck. It's made of flat metal and has holes that allow the truck to be attached to the skate deck.

Bearing
A hollow, round metal casing filled with greased ball bearings that attaches to a wheel. They make skateboard wheels spin.

Bolts
Two sets of nuts and bolts that attach the trucks to the skate deck.

Bowl
A combination of a shallow, round pool and a 360-degree mini-ramp.

Bushing
Small rubber circles that cushion the truck when it turns, located around the kingpin.

Coping
The lip at the top of a transition. On a ramp, it's the metal tube that joins the deck and the ramp. It is where grinds and slides are performed.

Deck
The top part of a ramp or a pool, which is where a skater stands before dropping in. Not to be confused with a skate deck.

Double Set
Two sets of stairs with a bit of flat ground between them on which a skater does tricks.

Filmer
Someone who films skateboarding with a video camera.

Flat Bar
A long, square rail, usually found at a skate park, that's laid about a foot (30 cm) off the ground, on which a skateboarder can grind or slide.

Flat Bottom (or Flat)
The flat part of the ramp, between the two transitions.

Flow Rider
A skater who gets free stuff from skate companies but doesn't make a living from skateboarding.

Front Foot
The foot that stays on the skate deck while the skater pushes. The front foot is, obviously, the foot that stays in front of the skater.

Frontside
A trick in which the rider leads up to the obstacle with the toes facing it.

Full Pipe
A completely rounded half pipe with no gaps in the surface other than the ends. Skaters just carve around in these.

Gap
The empty space between any two objects that a skateboarder jumps over. They can be the same height, or one can be higher than the other.

Graphics
The artwork on the bottom of a skate deck.

Grip Tape
Black sandpaper with glue on one side that is placed on the top of a skate deck for friction control.

Half Pipe (or Vert Ramp)
10- to 16-foot (3 to 4.9 m) high mini-ramps with an extended space between the transition and the coping.

Hanger
The part of a truck that hangs below the baseplate.

Hips
The sides of a pyramid. Two inclined planes meet without a flat part between them at anywhere from a 45- to 90-degree angle.

Hubba
The fat ledge down the side of a set of stairs.

Kingpin
The large bolt in the middle of a truck, which is tightened or loosened to determine the ease with which a skater can turn.

Launch Ramp (or Kickers)
These were and remain a mainstay of suburban skating, where there are often no skate parks or ramps. It's a small ramp skaters skate up to give themselves a bit of air so they can do flip or grab tricks.

Ledge
An obstacle normally made of concrete, granite or, ideally, marble on which skaters do grind or slide tricks.

Manny Pad
A large, flat, rectangular surface that skaters perform manuals on.

Mini-Ramp
They vary in size, but all mini ramps have the same characteristics: a flat bottom in the middle and transitions to coping on either side. A skater can do just about any trick on a mini.

Nose
The slightly less concaved end of a skate deck, which is pointed in front of the skater.

Pole
A traffic sign or a barrier pole that is bent enough so a skateboarder can skate it.

Pro
A skateboarder who makes a living from skateboarding and collects royalties from signature boards, shoes, wheels, trucks and clothing.

Pyramid
Mostly seen at skate parks, this obstacle is the same shape as the ones in Egypt, just at a less steep angle and with a flat top. Skaters use them to get height to do flip or grab tricks in midair.

Quarter Pipe
A transition that leads from flat ground to a coping. It looks like a mini-ramp cut into four quarters.

Rail
Handrails on staircases that skateboarders do tricks on or over.

Shop Rider
A shop-sponsored skateboarder.

Skateboard
The deck, trucks, wheels, bearings, bolts and grip tape completely assembled.

Skate Deck
The wooden board a skateboarder stands on.

Skate Tool
A multi-tool used to put together a skateboard. Designs vary but always include some sort of wrench.

Stair Set
A set of stairs at a skate park on which a skater does tricks.

Tail
The more concaved end of the skate deck, which faces behind the skater.

Team
A group of riders who represent a specific skateboard company.

Transition (or Tranny)
What makes a ramp a ramp. The transition is the curved part of the ramp, between the coping and the flat bottom. It's the part you'll be riding up on.

Truck
The metal devices attached to the bottom of a skateboard that allow it to turn.

Wallride
The act of skating up and on a stretch of wall.

Wheel
The four wheels that are attached to a skate deck.

Credits

Acknowledgments

First off, I'd like to thank myself for being so good-looking and talented. Life ain't easy when you're this pretty, so way to hang in there, beautiful.

Also, huge thanks to Harry Gils and Jeff Middleton, whose talent and dedication made this book look as good as its author does. No easy task.

To all the skaters whose input and patience made sure I got everything right: Scotty MacDonald (this should have been your book, chum. You can have the sequel), Chad Albert at Element Skateboards, Tomas Morrison, Morgan Smith and Brandon Del Bianco for letting Harry drag them out to do tricks that must bore them to tears. David Christian for the extra photos. Plus for good measure let's throw Dave Nolan in there. Yeah, I don't know why either, dude. 'Cause you're awesome?

Also, to all the skate companies who sent me free gear to include in this book — thanks for keeping me away from retail prices for another year. It's always greatly appreciated, guys.

Lastly, thanks to my Mom, Dad, Nan, and family (both genetic and extended). Oh, and to Dayna, who makes it all worthwhile.

Photo Credits

All photos by Harry Gils with the exception of the following:

David Christian 86, 96, 104, 116

Jeff Middleton 13 (deck with grip), 36 (red shoes)

Getty Images:
Bill Eppridge/Time Life Pictures 21 (right and left); V.J. Lovero/Sports Illustrated 22 (top); Richard Mackson/Sports Illustrated 22 (bottom right); Popperfoto 21 (bottom); Cameron Spencer 22 (bottom left).

Index